DOUBLE ELIMINATION

A BRIDGE MYSTERY

JIM PRIEBE

MASTER POINT PRESS
TORONTO - CANADA

Master Point Press
331 Douglas Ave.
Toronto, Ontario, Canada
M5M 1H2
(416) 781-0351
Website: http://www.masterpointpress.com
Email: info@masterpointpress.com

Library and Archives Canada Cataloguing in Publication

Priebe, Jim
    Double elimination : a bridge mystery / Jim Priebe.

ISBN 978-1-897106-30-3

    I. Title.

PS8631.R53D68 2007   C813'.6   C2007-905143-X

We acknowledge the financial support of the Government of Canada through the Book Publishing Industry Development Program (BPIDP) for our publishing activities.

Editor	Suzanne Hocking
Interior format & copy editing	Suzanne Hocking
Cover photo	©Paul Edmondson/Corbis
Cover and interior design	Olena S. Sullivan/New Mediatrix

Printed in Canada.

1 2 3 4 5 6 7   11 10 09 08 07

I wish to thank my wife, Joan, for her many, many reviews and comments on the evolving manuscript.

No one could have more supportive, enthusiastic colleagues than Ray and Suzanne at Master Point Press.

DOUBLE
ELIMINATION

A BRIDGE MYSTERY

CHAPTER 1

Art Fraser was not expecting a call. The blinking red light on his phone at the Reno Hilton puzzled him. He was on vacation and hardly anyone knew where he was. Deciding that the message was probably for his friend Karen, who was out of the room checking the afternoon bridge scores, he ignored it. Tossing aside the donut-shaped seat cushion that had been a constant companion to him since the accident, he lay down carefully and relaxed on the bed. Tender buttocks were no fun, even after a vast improvement over the past two weeks.

He felt a pleasant glow as he reviewed the bridge hand records showing the deals that he and his partner, Stewart Appleton, had played that afternoon. They had just completed the first final session of the Life Master Pairs in the 2004 Fall North American Championships, after finishing third among the qualifiers on the first day. He expected they were near the top today and would end up with a respectable placing.

Fraser had never had time to attend a national tournament before. He was able to do so now because the New York State police force allowed officers who had been wounded on duty to take up to three months medical leave. Fraser had been shot once in each buttock in the course of an investigation he had headed. During an early morning raid of a warehouse near Buffalo, they had arrested two suspects and were tracking down the third and final gang member. They had turned on all the warehouse lights and Fraser and a colleague had moved carefully through the aisles of the warehouse, crouching so as not to present much of a target to their quarry. As they duck-walked across the floor, they somehow moved ahead of the man they were after. Two shots rang out and Fraser felt a sharp, stabbing pain, first in his right buttock, then in his left. The first shot spun him around a few degrees and the second bullet entered the other side. Surprisingly, the pain was not nearly as excruciating as the embarrassment he felt every time he explained what had happened. The doctor told him that the wounds were not serious and neither muscle nor bone had been affected. He would be as good as new in no time.

Fraser quickly learned to appreciate the value of healthy buttocks for all the functions he had formerly taken for granted. He spent the first two weeks after the incident lying on his stomach. He turned on his side to eat and drink. Eventually he was able to sit for a short time, and then, with the help of his blessed thick foam pad, he was able to sit through a bridge game. His six-foot frame normally carried one-hundred-and-sixty-five lean pounds, but a month's forced inactivity combined with the leisure time he was taking now meant Fraser could feel the flab growing around his middle.

After the shooting, the police chief in charge of the Buffalo area, Gordon Bryder, had recounted the policy of allowing wounded officers three months medical leave and had wished him a speedy recovery.

"I have mixed feelings about this generous treatment we're giving you," said Bryder. "I'm a little suspicious about the way you got wounded. You know, some of the Mafia families have resorted to that method of punishment instead of outright killing."

"What method is that?" asked Fraser.

"They shoot the violator once in each cheek," said Bryder.

Fraser had been a bridge enthusiast since his college days. He enjoyed the weekly club games in Buffalo and had a good grasp of many of the finer technical points. His problem had always been that he didn't play frequently, and never with a really good partner, so he rarely had the opportunity to expose and correct his basic mistakes. All that changed with his injury, at least for a while. With plenty of time on his hands during his convalescence, he opted for total immersion. Frequent games, participation in after-game discussions and lengthy talks with Stewart Appleton, the manager of his favorite club, all led to a marked improvement in his play.

After four weeks of recuperation, and with ten weeks of leave remaining, Fraser broached the idea to his partner of going to Reno for a national tournament. Appleton turned the idea down at first, but he did call Susan Strong, a good friend and an expert partner from former days. When Susan showed enthusiasm for a Reno trip, Stewart changed his mind and two days later he told Art he was seriously interested.

For ten years, Art Fraser had been sharing an apartment with two other police officers — Jill and Karen. The three of them had been close friends since their time together at the New York State police academy. When the trio found themselves assigned to the same unit in Buffalo, they had agreed to take an apartment together. All three had been satisfied with the arrangement, or more precisely, no one had ever been dissatisfied enough to change it. Lately, though, Art had noticed Jill becoming less and less enthusiastic about matters. Karen had given him special attention during his convalescence, especially during the few days when he was totally immobile. Jill had observed this turn of events, and said nothing, but the awkwardness between them had continued to grow.

Unlike Jill, Karen was a keen bridge player. After Fraser's injury, they began playing together three or four times each week. She would need more training before she could realistically become a good tournament player, but she knew what she was doing and much of what she did worked well. Jill had never advanced beyond the beginner stage, and Art had lost interest in playing with her.

When Fraser came up with the notion of traveling to Reno, it was natural that he should ask Karen to accompany him. Equally natural was that Jill chose that day to announce her decision to leave. She told them the news before they left, including the fact that she would be gone when they returned. She wanted her own man and children. Fraser did not try to talk her out of the idea. He understood that the balance between the three of them had shifted. That was alright with him. He liked Karen better anyway.

Even though Karen moved quickly into the void left by Jill, Art often found himself considering what they might do to replace her. Finally, he chose a time to mention his thoughts to Karen over breakfast one morning in Reno.

"I think we should start looking for someone to move into Jill's old room," he said.

"You know what Dorothy Parker said?" inquired Karen.

"Who's Dorothy Parker?"

"Just a woman," responded Karen.

"Oh."

"A writer and poet who said many things better than anyone else ever did. She had sharp insights into the behavior of chauvinists."

"Do you know any chauvinists?"

"Yes, I do. The line I'm referring to goes like this.

> 'Woman likes monogamy
> Man prefers variety'

If you want to indulge your preference for variety, you'll have to do it without me. Just let me know and I'll leave right away. But if you want me to stay, there's something I need to make clear. It's time for monogamy. Jill was a special case. We both know that."

He knew better than to argue. *There are pluses,* thought Art. *They'll come to me.*

The lineups for the various bridge events were the subject of delicate negotiations. Art mentioned that he would be going with Karen and offered to play in whatever events Stewart wanted. They settled on playing as a foursome in a few team games, and agreed that Stewart and Art would play in two of the life master pairs events.

They all enjoyed Reno. They fared well in the team games. No one in the group had many masterpoints, so they avoided the highly competitive top brackets. Meanwhile, the weather was perfect, with many cloudless days, and the hotel service was excellent. Art felt that he was making the best of his holiday leave.

When Art learned that Karen was not expecting any phone calls, he decided it was time to deal with the blinking message light. Checking the message, he was surprised to find that it was Gordon Bryder who had called. Since it was late, he returned the call the next morning.

"Fraser! How are you feeling?"

"Better every day."

"Good. Glad to hear it. We need you up here."

"I'll be home next week. Monday, in fact."

"That's the earliest?"

"I bought one of those cheap excursion deals, and my airfare and hotel are all paid for in advance. You know how they work. If I change anything now, I get no refund and have to pay extra." Fraser thought he could sense Bryder's mind turning over, calculating what it would cost to bring him home early and the effect on the Genesee County police budget.

"We've uncovered a messy situation. We've dug up the bodies of a married couple who have been dead for a few years. Our pathologists identified them as Harry and Louise Lache. Do those names mean anything to you?"

"I knew a couple by that name a few years ago. They were good bridge players. Nobody's seen them around for ages."

"No wonder. They've been pushing daisies for three years at least, maybe four. Their bodies were dug up on Wellesley Island. They had a summer cottage there."

"That's a little outside our territory, isn't it?"

"The commissioner in Jefferson County, Sam Cameron, is an old friend of mine. We had our quarterly staff meeting in Albany this week and the case came up. He mentioned that the couple were well-known bridge players. I thought of you right away."

"Thanks, Chief," Fraser said dryly. "That's good of you."

"You're welcome. I'll arrange a temporary assignment to his unit."

"Don't they have any investigators of their own up there?"

"They have enough."

"So how come you're so keen to assign me to a case outside our county?"

"The state Commissioner likes to see cooperation between counties. He's had bad press lately for allowing fiefdoms to grow all over the state and he's pushing the idea of assigning you to the case. I'll get some brownie points out of this if it works. It won't hurt you either. If you solve this one, you'll get a lot of attention from the folks upstairs. I'm talking the good kind."

"It's hard to get excited about a four-year-old cold case. Is there any reason to think we can crack it now?"

"The bodies weren't around before. And of course, now we have a top sleuth on the job."

"I don't know who that could be. Alright, chief. Orders are orders, I guess. Can I at least choose my team?"

"Who did you have in mind?"

"I'd like to have Nelson and Wilson with me." Fraser thought fondly of the two detectives from Buffalo who had helped him solve the murder of two other bridge players a few years earlier.

"I can't do that. That would deplete the whole Genesee county criminal investigation unit. There won't be anyone left."

"Then this case can't be all that important to you."

"That's not the point. We need some staff here. You've been out of commission for several weeks. All the other guys are working extra to fill in for you. We can't spare the man power right now. The other two counties have agreed to supply some help."

"If Sam Cameron has the same mindset as someone else I know, I can just see his idea of help. A rookie and a pensioner. Why don't we put a time limit on the whole investigation? Maybe one week to finish the case. I'll have to work like hell, but I don't want to make a career out of a cold case like this. I have no idea what I'm getting into."

"Neither does anyone else. That goes with most murders. What you're asking makes sense, though. We'll cut it off at two weeks. I'll talk to Cameron up there and make sure he understands."

"You're so persuasive, Gordon. Sending me off to a territory where I don't know anyone, have no input into my team, to work on a case that's been sitting around for years. Okay. I fly in Monday and I'll be in the office on Tuesday, ready to roll to Wellesley Island by noon."

"Fine."

Art was not quite focused on the game that night, but he and Stewart finished in the top twenty, which they both considered respectable. They played in the North American Swiss with Karen and Susan on the final weekend, and made the cut at the halfway point. They were exactly average on the last day. Karen was excited about their performance.

"Thanks everyone for playing with me. I think that's a darn good finish. Top half of all North American players." Stewart and Susan just smiled.

CHAPTER 2

MONDAY, JULY 19, 1999

On a dank, drizzling morning in mid July of 1999, Harry Lache sat in his over-stuffed chair, thankful for the air conditioning in his sunroom, and thumbed through the *Erieville Daily Times* while sipping very good coffee. Rich food, washed down with plenty of good Bourbon and cheap red wine had combined with an easy lifestyle to transform Harry's once admirable abdominals into a decent-sized paunch. He loved the small town life of upper New York State. Twenty-five years ago, eighty thousand dollars of Louise's family money had been enough to buy a huge nineteenth century saltbox on a gorgeous lot. A few additional thousand helped them to renovate and maintain the structure in a more or less suitable style. Louise had plenty more where that came from, and Lache, nobody's dummy, was now earning a decent sum from the brokerage business he had been operating in Erieville during that time.

They spent most of their summer days at a cottage on Wellesley Island where they could entertain bridge-playing friends and play golf on one of two beautiful eighteen-hole courses. It would be hard to imagine a more handsome summer setting than Wellesley Island. The sparkling, icy Saint Lawrence River attracted only the hardiest guests for a swim, and local fishing required infinite patience, but from April to October, the island offered a sensation of clean, cool relaxation. With tasteful furnishings, five spacious guest bedrooms and an equal number of wash-rooms, the setup was admirable. The Laches were not gardeners and they did little to improve the property with formal flower beds. Lache made an effort to grow grass in front of the house. It grew well where the sun poked through, but was sparse for the most part. The bare spots were filled with ferns, Solomon's Seal, wild black raspberry and other native species. Their colors and minute crop helped to attract birds. Dense shade from the mature trees kept the whole property pleasant during most of the summer and the overall effect was delightful.

Everyone who visited was expected to pitch in with cooking and cleaning, but the Lache hospitality was superb and seldom did any of the regulars turn down an invitation to stay.

"What are the dates for San Antonio?" asked Harry.

"July twenty-first to August first," answered Louise. "We don't need to be there until the twenty-second. It's a three day drive, so we're leaving on the twentieth."

"We can make it in two days. It's only a thousand miles. There's nothing doing on the first Thursday anyway. Maybe a charity team game."

"If you're planning to drive to San Antonio in two days, I'm flying. You can take me to the Syracuse airport on the seventeenth and drive down yourself. You know damn well the trip is over eighteen hundred miles and we're going to take at least three days to drive it. Otherwise, I fly. And I want you to know that I happen to like the charity team games. I'll get team mates and meet you when you get there."

"I'm not taking time off if I don't need to. I have a business to look after. My customers are important. They may want to do a lot of trading."

"Trade all you want. Just take me to the airport. You only have three customers of any significance. They've been with you for years. Beth handles all the trades anyway."

Harry grunted, "Well, I give her specific instructions." He went back to his coffee and newspaper.

"How are Ron and Ted getting to San Antonio?" asked Louise.

"I don't know. That's their business," said Harry.

"It may be their business, but we could be courteous enough to offer them a ride."

"Ted's loaded. He doesn't need our charity. And I pay Ron Johnson enough that he can afford to fly. He shouldn't be taking all that time off anyway."

"My hard-nosed stockbroker. The guy who plays golf three days a week all summer."

"With customers."

"You've had the same customers for fifteen years. Why don't you try and cultivate some new customers some time?"

"These guys pay their bills. They pay a lot of our bills, too. Anyway, they're my friends. Every one of them has a big account."

"And Ron makes tons of money for them with his bond shenanigans."

"I don't know what you mean by shenanigans. He's a bond expert. A technician. One of the best around. But he couldn't cultivate a customer to save his life. I handle the business end."

"You can hardly complain about him taking time off for a bridge tournament. Our team would be a bunch of also-rans without him. We'd have a hard time getting someone as good if he decided to play elsewhere."

"Baloney. We play as well as any couple in the country. And I can keep Ted on the rails in our partnership. We could get a good fourth if we had to. You just said you'd easily get a team for the charity game."

"For regional events, it's much easier to get a decent team — you know that. I'm talking about national championship events. Ron and I have the best partnership on our team. We get to a lot of good contracts."

"Are you in love with the guy or something? He looks like a creep."

" What do looks have to do with it? You hired him. Nobody rates bridge players by their looks. He plays a hell of a lot better than either you or Ted. We won one national Swiss teams event. Ron and I made more good decisions on the final day than you guys did all week. We'd sputter away to nothing without him as my partner."

"Louise's scale of bridge expertise. I like that."

"Look. Let's not start a fight over nothing. You know very well we're driving together to San Antonio, and we're leaving on Tuesday. If you don't want to offer a lift to Ted and Ron, fine. But why did you get a car with a TV in the back seat if you were never going to take anyone for a ride?"

"It's just a conversation piece. A joke. The reception is terrible. You can't get any stations unless you're in a city, and if you're in a city, you don't want it on."

"Ron knows a ton of car games. He'd break up the monotony of the trip. But I'll go along with anything you want, as long as you allow three days for the drive."

She refilled Harry's coffee cup and he slid a hand under her housecoat.

"Careful! This pot is hot."

"So am I."

"Harry! The neighbors can see us."

"Good."

On Monday night, July 19, the night before the Lache's planned to leave for San Antonio, Harry was finishing the last of his packing for a two-week trip. He had planned his wardrobe for the full two weeks, knowing Louise would not be doing any laundry during the trip. Two large suitcases handled his needs and Louise herself had two more. The large trunk of his Cadillac swallowed everything without complaint. He would have liked room for his golf clubs, but knew he could rent a set in San Antonio if an opportunity arose for a game.

He had packed the last of their suitcases in the trunk and was slamming the lid when a friend walked up their laneway. "Hello, Harry," the visitor said.

"Come on in. I just packed the last suitcase for our trip tomorrow."

Those were the last words Harry ever spoke. The visitor, apparently accepting Harry's invitation for hospitality, followed him in the front door. Unseen by Harry, as soon as the front door closed, the visitor pulled a heavy instrument from a coat pocket and struck Harry on the back of the head. Harry fell heavily to the floor, unconscious.

Louise heard the commotion and rushed out into the hall.

"Oh. Hi," she said. "I thought I heard a noise." She noticed Harry slumped on the floor. "Oh dear," she gasped. "What —"

The visitor stepped forward and smashed her on the forehead, then quickly took a pillow from the living room chesterfield and held it forcibly over Harry's face until he had stopped breathing. The process was repeated on the prone body of Louise. To lessen the chance of interruption by other visitors, most of the lights in the house needed to be turned off. There was reason to be thankful for the large lot that made up the Lache property because it ensured that the house was not visible from the street. At this time of night, complete darkness blanketed the neighborhood and no one could observe the ugly performance taking place. A duffel bag stashed earlier at the front of the lawn held two large sleeping bags, each long enough to completely envelop an adult person. First Harry's body, and then Louise's, were stashed in the bags, which were then zipped up and dragged, with a mighty effort, one at a time to the back seat of Harry's car. Then the door was locked. Satisfied that there was nothing casually suspicious in the appearance of the back seat cargo, the visitor returned to the house, turned off all the lights, locked all of the doors, and casually drove the Cadillac out of the laneway and on to Interstate 81, heading north. The trip to Wellesley Island took one hour.

CHAPTER 3

MONDAY, MARCH 29, 2004

Fraser's plane took off at 7 a.m. on the Monday morning following the Reno tournament. He had a short layover in Denver and landed in Buffalo at noon. The flight was a long way from being comfortable. In spite of the cushion he had brought along, he had to get up every half hour and walk around as best he could. Karen barely suppressed a smile each time he rose.

"So you're going right back to a murder investigation?" she asked.

"Double murder, from the way Bryder talked. Did you ever know the Laches from Erieville?"

"I've heard the name, but not for years. I might have played against them a while ago."

"The story's gruesome. There was no trace of them until they dug up the bodies last week. Evidently, they'd been missing for four or five years. The Laches had no children. All of their estate went to a niece. She lives in Wisconsin somewhere. She finally got around to selling the cottage on Wellesley Island and the new owners decide to rip everything down. They do some excavating for a new foundation and these half-decayed corpses show up."

Karen made a horrified face. "And Bryder thinks this is a murder case?"

"Absolutely. The burial was strange. The killer evidently used sleeping bags for coffins, dug a shallow grave and buried them both there. The construction crew uncovered both bags. When the bulldozer dragged them up, the operator stopped to look into them and found human remains. The skulls of both victims showed signs of trauma."

"So why did the powers nominate you for the investigation? Wellesley Island is way out of our jurisdiction. The troops in Erieville won't like someone coming in from outside."

"Everything's on hold until I get there. The Laches were both bridge players, so Bryder thinks I'm the best man to assign to the case. He'll have to smooth things out with his counterpart up there. The two are old friends, evidently. They see each other periodically at staff meetings in Albany."

"You're not working the case all alone?"

"I asked him to assign Nelson and Wilson. He vetoed that one right away. Says it would decimate our group in Genesee County. I have zero input into the make-up of the team doing the investigation. I feel like a junior hired hand right now." He scowled and made to get up again. Karen leaned forward and put a hand on his arm.

"That's too bad. Your team worked well together on the Smithers' case."

"Maybe you could angle for an assignment to the criminal investigation branch?"

"Are you kidding? I love my job in traffic. Regular hours. No shootings behind my back."

"Very funny."

He went to find the drink cart.

The next morning Fraser eased himself into his red Firebird, smiling with satisfaction at the immediate growl the engine produced. The car was a close replica of the 1993 Indianapolis 500 pace car — a Camaro — and he dreamed of some day being a pace car driver in a major race. He took the familiar route to the police station at high speed, motivated partly by his resentment at the assignment he saw coming, and partly by a need to keep the time he spent on his backside to a minimum. It was easy to burn rubber, but Fraser was an excellent driver who knew his vehicle.

He thought about the upcoming meeting with Gordon Bryder. Fraser knew he had to fight his temper when dealing with colleagues. He had always disliked authority, and on the few occasions he had let his temper get the better of him, he had immediately wished he had kept his mouth shut. Although he liked Bryder and respected his position, Fraser was incensed at the idea of rushing off to someone else's territory to handle a cold case that hardly interested him. His thoughts during the drive wandered between anger at his situation and scheming how to turn matters to his own advantage. By the time he arrived in Bryder's office, he was in a calculating mood.

"Don't stand on ceremony," said Bryder with a smile. "Sit down and make yourself comfortable."

"I can't do both at the same time," replied Fraser, reaching over the desk to shake Bryder's hand.

"You could get a job teaching at the pistol range," suggested Bryder. "You can stand up all day on that job."

"Nice of you to think of my creature comforts, boss" said Fraser. "Can you tell me anything about the bodies they dug up on Wellesley Island?"

"You'll have to get that from the coroner up there. All I know is the bulldozer operator got a little ill when he saw what he had uncovered. We're pretty sure this is a bridge-related murder. That's why I want you on the job."

"You mean you want someone to navigate a bunch of blind alleys?" asked Fraser.

"You've been up a few, but you get your man. Listen, I can't tell you how to do your job, but if I were you, this is how I'd get started. First thing, head for Alex Cameron's office and introduce yourself. You'll like him. He's a good cop, been around a long time. Get him to tell you about the help he's giving you. Then you need to head up to the island and take a good look at the crime scene. You ought to stay a couple of nights up there and take the site apart."

"I thought we only knew that the bodies were buried there. Nobody says that the island is the crime scene."

"You're right," admitted Bryder.

"One of us, depending on who Cameron comes up with, needs to start talking to the people around there. The neighbors may know something. We'll have to interview them all. And we'll have to talk to people in Erieville, too. The murder scene may have been the Lache mansion for all we know. Or Lache's office. Chances are the whole thing will be over in a week. A trail gets cold after four or five years. Not many cases like these ever get solved. In my opinion, we've a snowball's chance of finding something useful."

Fraser's little speech effectively put a damper on the conversation. Bryder shrugged.

"Give it your best shot anyway. Our reputations are on the line, as usual."

"I'll do what I can with what I've got."

"Okay. But don't forget you can help yourself a lot by digging into this case.

Make sure you get along with Cameron. Get along with the guys he assigns to help. All of that will look good in your file."

"My file will have to look after itself. Nobody here, or in Albany or in Erieville, should have high hopes about solving this case. I can only promise you a professional effort. I can't promise to make our section look good."

"That's all I can ask for." Bryder sighed. "One last thing. Make sure you clarify expense accounting with Cameron right off the bat. I want everything, meals, hotels, gas mileage, all that stuff, to go against his budget, not mine."

"Naturally," said Fraser.

Fraser left the Buffalo headquarters of the New York State Police Department and headed for Erieville. The 220 miles took longer than normal because Fraser had to stop every hour to walk around and stretch. He arrived at the Jefferson county police headquarters at four o'clock. He walked in, introduced himself to the receptionist and asked for Alex Cameron's office. The receptionist was expecting him. She called to a Brad Macvey and a Stan Piper and two men ambled over.

Although Piper and Macvey were native to the Erieville region, they were a study in contrasts. Piper was small, with an air of quickness and neatness. He had a carefully trimmed Charlie Chaplin moustache and wore a worn, well-fitting suit, a white shirt and an obviously dated narrow red silk tie. His movements and appearance gave the impression that he was about to lurch off unexpectedly in some direction to carry out an urgent, unknown task. Macvey, on the other hand, was dressed carelessly in his blue and gold state trooper uniform, shirt barely tucked in at the waist, with unruly red hair and a trace of good humor in his blue eyes. His build was burly and his movements were bear-like, suggesting power, with little wasted motion.

"Glad to meet you," said Macvey. "I'm looking forward to some real work. It's boring as hell up there standing guard on the murder site."

"I can imagine," said Fraser. "How long have you been on this job?"

"Since last week. About ten days in all. Stan spells me off overnight."

Fraser turned to the older man. "Are you bored as hell, too?" Fraser asked.

"I look after myself," said Stan. "I'm a realist about these assignments."

He's not about to complain in front of his boss, thought Fraser. *Macvey seems a little impatient. Maybe that's good.* "Two of you looking after the site. That's a lot of manpower," he said.

"Nobody's there now," said Macvey. "We came down for the big introduction. And there's not a damn thing I can do when I'm tied up there."

"Were you around when the bodies were found?" Fraser asked of Macvey.

"I wasn't involved right at the start. Later, the chief asked me make a list of neighbors and talk to everyone close. I talked to a few of the neighbors, but got nothing useful."

"I'll take all you've got," said Fraser.

"I'll pass on my file. Don't get your hopes up."

Fraser thought, *with this lack of enthusiasm, we're going to have the case finished in a hurry.* Then he realized he must have sounded exactly the same himself when he talked to Bryder.

Fraser looked at the list Macvey had compiled of the Laches' Erieville neighbors. He had included a small, hand-drawn map, coated in donut sugar, which noted names and locations for about ten families in all. "You've talked to all of these folks?" asked Fraser.

"Yep. Everything's in the files. Some of them have been there longer than the Laches. Some just moved in. I don't think there's anyone who can help much. They're mostly mild people, long-time Erieville residents. They'd no more think of killing someone than flying to the moon. None of them was all that close to the Laches. Same story all over. They liked the missus and not the old man."

"None of them was good friends with the Laches?"

"Not a single one. The Laches had their own bunch, and that didn't include the neighbors."

After a quick glance at the file Macvey had produced, Fraser said, "I'll take this, if you don't mind. I can look at it tonight. You haven't talked to anyone on the island?"

"Not yet. Our job was to look after the property on the island, make sure nobody disturbed anything. I have a list of homeowners on the island, but the only folks I've talked to are the ones in Erieville."

"Where do you guys live?" asked Fraser.

Macvey came from a small town near Syracuse and Piper lived in a hamlet on

Lake Ontario, about thirty miles northwest of Erieville.

"So neither of you lives in Erieville," Fraser said. "We'll have to find a place to stay around here. Okay. I need a few minutes alone with Cameron to discuss arrangements and we'll get going."

Macvey offered to set up an appointment with the coroner as soon as they finished with Cameron and walked away to arrange it.

Fraser moved into Alex Cameron's office and took the liberty of closing the door behind him. Cameron was a big man with a friendly air. He dislodged his bulk slowly from his chair and moved to shake hands. "Glad you could make it up here," said Cameron in a deep, impressive voice. "We've been having a hell of a time trying to figure this one out. We're nowhere at the moment and it'll take a good man to crack it. A very good man."

Seated across from Cameron was a lady whom Fraser judged to be in her early forties. Her hair was graying in spots. She wore no makeup and her clothing was dark and expensive. A quick smile accentuated by dimples on each cheek relieved the severity of her appearance. Cameron introduced her as Diana Westbury, district attorney of Jefferson County. She and Cameron had just concluded a meeting, and Cameron had asked her to stay on to meet Fraser.

She smiled. "Glad to see you on the case."

"Thanks," said Fraser. "I'm not quite sure what I'm getting into."

"I know what you mean. We appreciate any help you give us. I never interfere with Sam's work, but I'm always available for a consultation." She gave Art a business card and rose to leave. "Call me anytime — at the office or my cell phone. I'll be glad to hear from you whenever you think it's important." She stood up. "I'll let you two carry on. Good luck, Art." She shook hands with both men and left.

"I hope I can do some good here," said Fraser, grimacing as he sat down, wishing he had remembered to bring his air cushion. "The odds are against us."

"I know all about it. But they're better now that you're with us. I'm happy Gordon wanted to cooperate. Can I do anything to help?"

"There are a couple of things. Gordon says he's leaving me here for two weeks, and then I go home. He said you'd assign a couple of detectives to the case."

"No problem there. You've met Brad Macvey and Stan Piper already."

"Brad's a fine officer, I'm sure," said Fraser. "He's not a detective."

"He's a smart young fellow. Knows the area and the people. I don't have anyone else free right now. Stan was a detective. He's in his late sixties, but he still has plenty to offer."

"I assume Brad is available full time."

Cameron grimaced, and nodded his assent. "He's a keen lad. You don't want to turn him off. He knows a lot about the island."

Fraser nodded and continued. "What's Stan's background? What kind of work did he do as a detective?"

"He's a retiree, on an hourly contract. We don't have the extra manpower sitting around. I took the trouble to set him up with a contract specially to help on this case. He was a pretty good man at tracking down robbers. We assigned him to several theft investigations over the years."

"As lead man?"

"No."

"I'd really prefer to work with someone with a background in homicide. If I have to train two novices, one of them seventy years old, I start with two strikes against me."

"Just a minute now," countered Cameron. "I said late sixties, not seventy. And what make you think you need to train anyone? I've known Stan for twenty years. He's well trained and reliable. Let's not jump to conclusions."

"He has no experience in homicide. You said so yourself."

"Stan will do a good job for you," said Cameron. He regained his strong voice. "Here's how it is. You have two choices. Take him and Macvey or take Macvey. Matter of fact, you can make it three choices. Do the whole thing yourself, if that's what you want." The facade of friendliness had crumbled.

Fraser absorbed this final note without offering an immediate response. His worst fears about the quality of his help seemed to be materializing, Anger surged, and he felt powerless to control the important aspects of this assignment. Then he reminded himself of the words spoken by Jim Kesten, his boss of a few years ago, cautioning him that he had a reputation as a hothead. *You make enemies quickly and permanently. No man is a success as a captain unless he gets people on his side. If you build up animosity in your colleagues, you'll be a loser.* The right course of action was to put a positive spin on matters. He asked, "When the Laches were reported as missing, what kind of investigation did you lay on at the time?"

"They just vanished four years ago. We found they were headed off on a trip to Texas, for some bridge tournament. They were never heard of again, until this past week. The car still hasn't turned up. A '95 Cadillac. Everybody figured they must have had an accident somewhere on route."

"Did you talk to the people in Lache's firm?"

"He had a couple of employees. One of them reported the couple missing, matter of fact. The business is still going and the two employees still run it. We talked to the two folks there and everybody else we could think of. Golf buddies. Bridge players. Harry's friends and customers were all from those bunches. They have no kids and no close relatives. We couldn't uncover anything useful at all."

"So I'm starting at ground zero," said Fraser. Cameron nodded.

"I assume you can give Stan Piper a car for the duration."

Cameron grimaced again. "He's been charging us mileage for use of his own car. He prefers that. As a matter of fact, he drives a BMW."

"Really? Your retirees do alright."

"The rules say he can get a standard mileage allowance. He bought the thing second hand. It's a 1990 model, but he keeps it in perfect condition. Like I say, I've known him a long time. I'd advise you not to discount Stan. He's honest and he's a bulldog."

"What about Macvey?"

"He's driving a local rental unit. He can keep that as long as he needs it for official business. He needs to turn it in weekends if you're not working overtime."

"And what facilities can we make use of here?"

"We have three rooms here for common use of all officers. Interviews, meetings, whatever. I can't give you a private office, but there's always a room or two free here. Just make yourself at home."

"I'll do that."

"There is a final point I need to cover with you. An old hand like you will understand what I'm getting at. We don't have big budgets up here like you fellows do in the big cities. I have to watch expenses pretty closely. I'd like to ask your cooperation. No unnecessary expenses to unload on the taxpayers." Cameron's smile reappeared.

Fraser thought, *like hiring retirees, paying for BMW mileage and rental cars.* "I assume you'll have no problem covering meals, accommodation and any other incidentals we pay for. The mileage on my car goes on my expense account as well." He looked straight into Cameron's eyes as he spoke, and laughed inwardly as the smile faltered, then vanished, and was finally replaced with a strained imitation.

"I'm just asking you to be reasonable about it." Cameron did not rise as Fraser thanked him and left to rejoin Macvey and Piper.

"How far to the coroner's office?" asked Fraser.

"Five minutes," Macvey said. "He lives just north of here. He'll see us right away."

Doc Atlee was ready as advertised. Brusque and all business, he brought out photographs of the excavation and a stuffed file folder. "I personally supervised the digging. The bulldozer operator uncovered a sleeping bag. Ripped the cloth and then saw body parts exposed. He stopped and called his boss, who let the police know. I got up there later in the day. Made them do the rest of the digging by hand. We found a second sleeping bag with a body inside. That one didn't get ripped up. Look, here's the log I made. I wrote down everything we did and what we found. I've got pictures, too. You'd better look at them. They're not pretty. I doubt anyone except the prosecutor and the judge will want to look closely at them.

"The bodies were down there several years — I guess four or five going by what people say was the last time anyone talked to them. Body tissue in the ground doesn't break down as fast as it does in air. The eyes go quickly and you have hollow sockets. The rest takes a surprising time to decay. No predators get at it, and there's very little oxygen down there to help decomposition. They were fully dressed and zipped up in sleeping bags, so all those factors combined would really slow down the decaying process. The flesh was a bit gone, I guess, but really just starting to decompose.

"I carted the remains up to the forensic lab in Albany in my van. I wasn't letting anybody else lose them or damage them, so I took them myself. You can't find volunteers to truck bodies around anyhow. Not without a casket. The lab can't pin down the time of death, but they did give us a positive ID from dental records. Harry and Louise Lache. The property went to a niece until she sold it a couple months ago. The lab also confirms that this is a case of murder and that the weapon was a blunt, heavy instrument of some sort."

"Did anyone contact the niece?"

"We got hold of her and gave her the bad news. She came to town last week to look after the funeral. Nice lady."

"What about the scene of the murder?" asked Fraser. "Was there anything around you can tell us about?"

"You guys are going to have to figure that out yourselves. There's nothing left of the summer house the Laches had on that site. It was demolished and the rubble carted off weeks ago. The bulldozer operator was excavating for the place the new owner planned to build."

"So all we've got from the site is the remains of our two victims. Nothing else." Fraser rubbed his temples.

"That's right, my friend," Doc Atlee said. "Nothing else. If I were you, I wouldn't jump too quickly to the conclusion that the island property was the murder site. My guess is the murder took place in Erieville and the bodies were disposed of up there."

"That makes sense," said Fraser. "We'd better move on. I'm sure you have lots to do here."

"Call me any time. I'll be glad to do whatever I can."

After they left the coroner, Fraser addressed Macvey and Piper. "I'd like to see the property on the island where the bodies were found. Can we do that tonight?" His partners nodded assent and he continued. "We've also got to work out a way to set up shop. We need to consult regularly until this thing takes shape. It looks like our time will be split between Erieville and Wellesley Island. We'll have an hour's drive either way. We should all stay in the same motel. What do you suggest, here or the island?"

"I say we start at the island," said Macvey. "That's where the bodies were found and we'll probably find out more up there. We can always move after a week or so."

Fraser did not let on that he was hoping to pull out of the area and return to Buffalo after two weeks. Piper indicated with a wordless shrug that he was flexible.

Macvey cleared his throat. "The only thing is I want to get to Syracuse this weekend. I got a girl there and I want to see her on the weekend, at least."

"That should work," affirmed Fraser. "Do either of you know anything about motels on the island?"

Macvey said, "There's an old hotel near the bridge and a fairly modern motel near the golf club. They're both decent and both serve food."

"Which one do you recommend?" asked Fraser.

"I'd take the motel at the golf course."

"Will Cameron like the bill we send him?"

"Cameron will complain anyway. Now that I think about it, the hotel probably isn't open yet anyway. They only open it for summer tourists. So we have no choice. It'll be off season at the motel, so rates will be low."

"OK. Let's do that. We can meet here in the station when we need to. Otherwise, we'll get together on the island. We'll float around back and forth a lot until we sort a few things out. Bring along your list and the map so we can work out a plan to call on all the neighbors over the next couple of days," said Fraser. "One of us will have to pay a visit to the office where Lache ran his business, track down where he bought his car, and so on. That means someone will have to travel to Erieville while the others are looking around the island."

"He drove a Cadillac, the car that went missing. There's a Cadillac dealer in Erieville," said Macvey.

"Good. I'd like to talk to him."

Macvey and Piper agreed to join Fraser for supper to help plan their approach to the investigation. They all drove separately to their motel on Wellesley Island, checked in, and went to visit the former Lache property. Macvey led them around and showed the excavations for the foundation of a new building. The small bulldozer was still on the site.

"The contractor's been bugging me about letting him move his equipment. He says he pays a hundred bucks a day to rent it. I told him we can do that after the chief okays it."

"No need to keep it around, is there?" asked Fraser.

"That's your call. I didn't want him moving anything we might need to look at."

"Let's take a peek. We can release it today if we don't find anything."

"You saw the photos of the bones Doc Atlee had. The tractor mashed up the first ones they found pretty good. The bulldozer operator knew enough to stop everything as soon as he realized what he was digging up. At first he couldn't tell what was going on. Animal bones are all over around here. When he saw a skull he got pretty scared. That's when he stopped everything and called us. I came up with Cameron and we called the doc as soon as we saw the bones. He took charge after that."

Before he retired, Fraser took out the file of Erieville neighbors that Macvey had given him. The notes were done in messy handwriting, but the information was neatly arranged and the notes corresponded logically with the equally messy map. He looked up neighbors on both sides of the street and on either side of the Lache house. The dates when people had moved in to the area were all faithfully record-ed, as well as a log of information recording the dates that previous owners had moved out. *This guy is thorough,* thought Fraser. *I didn't suspect it.*

CHAPTER 4

Wednesday morning, Fraser asked Stan Piper to interview the employees at the stock brokerage firm that Harry Lache had owned in Erieville. Meanwhile, he asked Brad Macvey to stay on the island and talk to as many neighbors as he could find. Fraser took on himself the task of calling on the Cadillac dealer in Erieville. The salesman he talked to was able to provide a serial number for the Cadillac the Laches owned, as well as a detailed description of the equipment. He contacted Mike Eppler, a long time colleague at police headquarters in Albany, and requested a nationwide alert for the vehicle.

"I don't mind doing that right away, Art," said Mike. "You know what our chances are of finding a vehicle with a four-year-old license number on a nationwide alert."

"Yeah, but I've got to start somewhere."

"If you could pin anything down — the area, the date."

"I'll work on it, Mike. We can pin down the date when it disappeared. I'll pass that on to you. I'll look into possible locations, but that'll be a wild-ass guess."

He hung up and dialed the number of an old contact in Buffalo. Al Finestone had been a witness in a case that Fraser brought to trial while in the vehicle investigation unit in Buffalo. Al had been up for arrest in the case, but Fraser had seen the affair clearly and gotten him off the hook quickly. Al, surprised and grateful, passed on his phone number and offered to help Fraser whenever he might need it. Fraser thought it was time to cash in on this offer. Surprisingly, he got through on the second ring.

"Hi, Al. It's Art Fraser."

"I thought you gave up cars for an easier racket."

"Old habits die hard. Listen, where would a stolen '98 Cadillac Eldorado likely end up? They wouldn't bust one of those up for parts, would they?"

"What's it worth to you?"

"You owe me one. More than one, as a matter of fact."

"That was yesterday. This is today. Okay. A car like that, they wouldn't ship it very far. They wouldn't break it up either. It's not that big a seller. Parts would-n't be worth much. But in one piece, in good shape, they might paint it up and hustle it."

"Where? Your best guess."

"South. Not in California. Not the West. My best guess? I'd say anywhere in Florida. Or it could be Mississippi, Alabama, the southern part. Right along the gulf. Lots of them there."

"Okay, Al. What about a body shop down there that would do the paint job?"

"You expect me to know that? Get serious. You know the game. Forget the dealers. Forget the franchises. They wouldn't touch it. You're left with independ-ent body shops. There aren't that many. Get into the back woods of Alabama and Mississippi and you get shops stuck where nobody ever sees them. They could do any number of your Caddies and no one would ever know."

"So your best guess is somewhere along the gulf?"

"What do I know? They love big Caddies down there and they don't really care how old they are. They don't use salt on the roads and cars never rust out. I gotta go. I'm expecting a call."

"We're done anyway. Thanks."

"I'd say we're even now."

"Not quite. But this may help. So long."

Brad Macvey skipped breakfast with his colleagues to phone his girlfriend, Sophie, in Syracuse. After assuring her he would be back in time for Sophie's birthday din-ner on Saturday, he ordered a cup of black coffee, a couple of muffins and drove to the neighborhood he was going to inspect. It was a beautiful day without a cloud in the sky. Macvey opened the sunroof on his car to take advantage of the exhilarating air. He parked near the cottage, pulled out the map on which he had scribbled the names of neighbors, and settled in to study it.

What happened next would shame and embarrass him for many years to come. He would be forced to laugh it off countless times before his friends and coworkers would get tired of the story. Even as he sat in the car, enjoying his treat, a flock of half a dozen wild turkeys was roaming the neighborhood, foraging for food along the side of the road. Food was still scarce in the early spring and the birds were hungry. A pair of gobblers, probably averaging thirty pounds each, approached Macvey's car. They caught his attention when they jumped up on the hood. He leaned forward to examine them more closely. *About as ugly as you can get,* he thought. One of the pair eyed Macvey's partly eaten muffin and unsuccessfully tried to retrieve it by banging its head on the windshield. While Macvey was distracted looking into the face of the first bird, the adventurous partner hopped on to the top of the car and entered through the sunroof. Man and bird were both stunned to be in such close quarters together. Both reacted instinctively. The natural instinct of the bird was to target the eyes of its enemy. Macvey put up a vigorous defense and for a few moments thought he was in for really serious injury. Macvey was never a man to panic, but when the bird displayed a frightening vocabulary of piercing sounds, he came close. He flailed at the bird with one hand and tried to open the car door with the other. By the time he got himself out of the car, the bird had ripped his face in several places and he was bleeding. When the bird was finally out of the car and Brad had chased it off, he contacted the motel and asked for the location of a nearby doctor's office.

"What's up?" asked the clerk when Brad arrived with a napkin held to his face.

"I had a little accident. Nothing serious."

The injuries were indeed painful, but more conspicuous than serious. An observer might have been fooled into thinking that they were life threatening. Three of them required stitches and the doctor gave him a tetanus shot. He returned to his car looking like a good candidate for a part in a Boris Karloff movie. He reckoned that a philosophical attitude was the only way to deal with the encounter, and it was after 11 a.m. by the time he made it back to the Lache lot and parked. He took out his map once again and worked out a plan. There were five names to check out: two on the Lache side and three across the street. The smallest lot in the area was over an acre in size and the Lache section, one of the largest, was over five acres. Macvey could see that it was going to take a great deal of tramping to complete his calls. Neither of the adjacent neighbors was home, so he tried the house directly across the street. No one answered his knock, but since there was a car in the laneway, he decided to go around to the back of the house. When the back garden came into view, he was greeted by a pair of buttocks clad in blue denim moving vigorously from side to side to the accompaniment of grunts and an exhortation to "C'mon out you son of a bitch."

Macvey walked over to the straining woman and asked, "Can I help?"

The woman took a furtive look behind her, saw Macvey with his bandaged face, decided that what she saw was a threat, and lurched at him with her shovel. Macvey, a veteran of a good deal of physical combat, with training as well as experience, generally came out a winner. A woman with a shovel was a brand new challenge, however. With the element of surprise on her side, she managed to land one solid blow on his right shoulder before he could help her lower the shovel, gently, and hold her hands firmly, while he explained who he was. He apologized for his appearance and mentioned that he had had an accident earlier in the day.

The husky woman turned out to be Lucy Dinde. He judged her to be in her mid-fifties. Faded denims spotted with dried mud suggested that she was accustomed to heavy labor. She was now reasonably calm and Macvey felt safe in releasing her wrists.

"Can I take that thing out for you?" he asked.

Surprised, she said, "Give it a try if you want."

With his bruised shoulder forgotten for the moment, Macvey took hold of the offensive shrub with both hands, did a little grunting and straining of his own, and managed to dislodge the remainder of its roots. "There," he said, feeling the pain return to his shoulder.

The lady said admiringly, "My, you are strong. Thanks a lot. That damned thing was giving me fits. Say, you want a coffee?"

Macvey began to feel a little less self-conscious about his appearance, as the woman was obviously warming to him. "That would be great. Black, please."

Lucy disappeared into the kitchen and returned a few minutes later. When he saw the good-sized plate of oatmeal cookies she carried, he forgot his combined injuries once again and found that his appetite had quickly returned.

"Did you know the Laches?" he blurted between bits of oatmeal.

"Of course I knew them," she answered. "They haven't been up here for years. I was surprised at that. They loved it here."

"You didn't know they died?"

She gasped. "When was that? Did they have an accident or something?"

"That's what we're looking into," explained Macvey. "Their bodies were dug up when the guy with the bulldozer got going."

"Don't tell me."

"I need you to pass on everything you can. How well did you know them?"

"We weren't close. I guess you'd say they were good neighbors. I saw a lot of them the first summer they were up here. Harry was an asshole. She was okay. They were great bridge players, you know."

"I heard that, yeah."

"They played bridge every night. They used to invite me over all the time. Harry and Louise, and this young creep called Ron Johnson, he came up on weekends. And an old guy called Ted. He and Harry were good friends. They used to play for pretty high stakes. More than I could afford. I lost almost a thousand dollars one night, and that finished me with them."

"They were that good?" asked Macvey.

"I never thought they were that much better. Louise was always very nice. I was getting to like her. But Harry. I couldn't stand him. When he played with Ted Lugner, I swear they were cheating. When they played as partners, they used to make these phony bids — psychic bids they call them. I never knew what was going on. They'd talk me out of a game or a slam and laugh their heads off. And they talked so much. You're not supposed to talk during the game. It's okay after the hand is finished, but not while you're bidding or playing. They yakked away. I'm sure they were passing information across to one another. That last night, I just decided to quit."

"When did you last see them?"

"Oh, I can hardly remember. I lost track. Four or five years ago. They just disappeared. Then their place went up for sale. I guess the new owner didn't like it and tore it down."

"How about the people that bought the place. Ever meet them?"

"No, just picked up some gossip. A rich guy. Must be rich to tear down Lache's old place and afford a new, bigger one. The Lache place was nice inside and out. I would have been very happy with it. Some hardwood floors and the rest beautiful vinyl. Nice furniture, too."

"What about suspicious stuff happening over the years at the Lache place? Did you see anything at all?"

"Oh boy. Four years ago. Or is it five? Come to think of it, it's strange that the house sat empty for years and then all of a sudden somebody bought it. So they've been dead all along?" Macvey nodded. "Well one thing that puzzled me was I remember Dan Gehl, he lives right next door, I saw him one day around the place. The Lache place, I mean. I thought that was pretty funny. He went right in and carried some stuff out. Heavy stuff, like furniture. He carried it out and hustled it over to his place. I assumed he bought it. That was a while ago. It happened right after the Laches stopped coming up here."

"Did you ask him about it?"

"Oh no. I mind my own business. I wasn't getting into that."

"Was he the only one you ever saw going into the place?"

"I'd say so. The Laches always kept the place in pretty good shape. Not much of a lawn with all the trees, but it was always tidy. Then it seemed to go all wild. I mean, it was nice enough, but not like they anyone was keeping it trimmed. Nobody came around to do any work in the yard. I'm out all the time in mine. I love gardening."

"What about the neighbors? I tried a couple of houses and nobody was home. Do they all live here year round? Or do they just come in the summers?"

"Gehl lives here all year. The Burnies, they're in the little place right across the street. They only come here in July and August. Their home is just a summer place. The Walkers are year-rounders, and who's the other one? Oh yeah. The Hills. They're a strange couple. They have a beautiful place. They come here any-time — summer, winter, you name it. They never stay long."

"Why strange?"

"They pick odd times to come here. The weather can be rainy in the summer, and here come the Hills. Maybe it's miserable in the winter. We get pretty good winters here. They show up when it's freezing."

"Were the Hills friends of the Laches?"

"Oh yes. They spent a lot of time together."

"Did the Laches have a lot of visitors?"

"I wouldn't say a lot. They always had the same crowd. They'd invite a few friends and play bridge for a whole weekend. You might see Harry out barbecu-ing, or maybe someone going for a walk, but that's it."

Macvey finished his coffee, thanked Lucy, gave her his card and said, "Call me if you think of anything. We'll be nosing around the neighborhood for a while. I'll drop by again next week."

"I've got a few more of them stumps to come out, if you're interested," said Lucy, smiling.

Macvey stretched his shoulders as he got into his car. He was beginning to feel a dull ache in the spot where Lucy had pummeled him with the shovel and he could sense a good bruise developing. He referred to his map and looked at other names along the road. He drove slowly, trying to determine if anyone else was home, finally spotting signs of activity at a poor-looking shack. The laneway was not paved and he had to skirt along its edge to avoid mud and small pools of dirty water. The paint on the clapboard house was not new, but it was in good condition. A few blows on the door brought a rustle of feet, loud barking, and some snarling from inside. Shouts of "Shut up" and "Get down, damn you" came from inside. Then a small, unshaven, older man appeared in the doorway.

"What'n hell do you want?"

Macvey was beginning to feel that the island's inhabitants were naturally offended by the sight of a stranger. He sensed that his bandaged face and drooping right shoulder might have a little to do with this. All he could do was produce his police identification and introduce himself, restraining the urge to pick the little fellow up and prop him in a chair for a lecture. To accomplish this, he would have had to deal first with the trio of dogs that seemed to be everywhere. One jumped on the front of his thighs, another grabbed a trouser cuff and threatened to tear it off, while the third launched a flank attack and almost knocked him over. As it happened, Macvey was a dog lover and handled the attackers like an expert. He managed to pat each of them in turn and say a few words in a friendly tone to calm them down. A few oaths from the little old man got them out of the way and Macvey confirmed that the man's name was Dan Gehl.

Gehl looked to be in his late seventies or early eighties, but moved briskly, displaying the agility of a person who has spent much of his life outdoors. His place was a mess and his appearance was equally untidy. It seemed that he was his own man, shared and understood only by his three dogs.

"Macvey. I know that name. There was Macveys on the island years ago."

"That'd be my great grandfather," said Brad.

"You're one of them, are you? My daddy worked with one. That's your great grandfather?"

"I suppose."

"Small world. They were both stone masons."

"So I've heard. I never met him."

"Worked on Boldt castle around 1900 for a few years. They stopped everything when old lady Boldt died."

"I remember that story."

"Well, come on in. I suppose you're here about the Laches?"

"That's right. You knew them well?"

"Sure. I worked for old Harry plenty. Did his lawns and odd jobs. He paid me pretty good, too."

"Did you know Mrs. Lache?"

"Sure. She was a looker when she was younger. She was always good to me. I liked her. Too bad about the way Harry carried on."

"What do you mean?" asked Brad.

"Well, there was a time when he went after that Dinde woman. They went at it hot and heavy for a few months. I seen him go over to her place in broad daylight and come out a couple of hours later. Mrs. Lache must have known about it. She couldn't miss it. She always took things pretty cool. Never saw her lose it. One time we had a big storm. Knocked a tree over their roof, broke the ridge beam. You know what that is? The main beam up there. Anyway, cracked that and broke the roof wide open. Wrecked stuff inside. Rugs and furniture. She just called me up and says can you fix it? Well, I'm a pretty good carpenter. I tell her I can fix the house but not the furniture. She says fine, so I hired a couple guys and we fixed it. She stayed calm the whole time."

Brad pressed on. "You say Mr. Lache had a thing going with Lucy Dinde?"

"Lucy, is it? Like I say, for maybe a whole summer. Then something happened and they stopped seeing each other. I never saw Mrs. Dinde go over for a visit again."

On his way back to his car Macvey wrestled once more with the dogs and then found he had to forcibly restrain them to prevent them from jumping into his car for a ride.

While Brad Macvey was discovering the dangers of wild turkeys and shovel-wielding gardeners on Wellesley Island, Stan Piper was driving to Erieville to carry out his assignment at the former office of Harold Lache, Investment Counselors. He was glad to be off by himself and set to the project with enthusiasm. He was a loner by nature and nothing could beat getting off by himself, especially, if he could find a subject jam-packed with minute details. The opportunity to lose himself in the finer points of an investigation made him feel like a whole man. He liked to keep copious records in a small notebook that never left his possession. Every entry was printed in a neat, legible hand, dated and spiced with all of the details that Stan thought might be of use at some future date. He had many such books in his home, which he planned to open once he got a little free time.

He arrived before the building was open for business and walked up and down the street to gauge the surroundings. He made a note of an attractive, athletic lady in her late thirties or early forties, wearing a dark blue skirt and a matching blue jacket, who entered the premises at 9:05 a.m. A thin, stooped man in his late forties wearing jeans and an overlarge sweater followed ten minutes later. After looking around for a few more minutes, Stan entered the building.

He walked over to the woman and in an offer to shake hands unsuspectingly let her grasp the ends of his fingers. She responded with a crushing grip that produced, in quick sequence, a sharp pain, an involuntary gasp and finally the trace of a smirk on a normally unsmiling face. Every aspect of Beth Harper's appearance, set face, absence of makeup and dark, unfashionable clothes, reinforced an impression of severity. Nevertheless, Stan found her unusually attractive and couldn't help wondering if she had remained unmarried in a small town like Erieville.

"Stan Piper," he said, introducing himself.

"Beth Harper," she said, adding, "Miss Beth Harper," which answered his curiosity.

"You have a fair grip," he remarked, working his fingers to reduce the stabbing pain he was feeling.

"That's from holding a tennis racquet," answered Beth. "I play four nights a week, sometimes five. We have a great club here."

Piper felt himself overcome by a wish that he had taken up tennis earlier in life. Too late now, of course. Perhaps he could find another angle to get to know Miss Harper better. The subject deserved serious thought.

With his fingers still throbbing, he turned to the gentleman in the office. He approached Ron Johnson with caution, but the man surprised him with a limp handshake and an averted glance as they mumbled names. Johnson wore the casual uniform that bridge players favored, where anyone who dressed neatly stood out as either a professional, a rich client or a league official. Unruly blond hair, thick glasses, and a saggy cotton sweater completed the image of a man suited to a life of studying bridge hands and bond yield curves.

Stan asked the pair if he could talk to them together and then interview each separately. Ron Johnson showed him into a small conference room with walnut paneling and leather upholstered hairs. Beth served up three cups of coffee. Stan introduced his task by asking what they knew about Harry and Louise Lache.

"Harry owned the place, of course," said Johnson, taking the lead in responding. "We both knew him well. Beth here has been around longer than I have. We were shocked to learn that their bodies were found up near the old cottage."

"The Laches gave me this job, and it's all I ever wanted to do," said Beth. "I love it here. I've lived in Erieville all my life."

"How did you hear about the Laches' deaths?" asked Stan.

Once again, Johnson was first to answer. "We read about it in the Erieville Times several days ago. You might say we've been expecting to read something like it sometime. They disappeared almost four years ago, in the summer. Personally, I thought they had a car accident somewhere. They were on their way to San Antonio in July of '99. I was supposed to meet them there, but they never showed up. Nobody heard of them again until the article came out in the newspaper. The paper is saying it was murder."

"It was a real shock," added Beth.

"So the first you heard of their deaths was in the Erieville newspaper?" asked Stan.

"Yes," agreed the pair.

Stan arranged to spend an hour with Johnson that morning. Johnson was friendly and cooperative, but added little to the limited information Stan had already acquired.

"You've been here almost twenty-five years?"

"It'll be twenty-six in June. I graduated in '78 and Harry gave me a job right out of school. I've never worked anywhere else."

"You came here right out of college?"

"That's right. I finished my MBA at Cornell and came right here. I met Harry that spring when he came to Cornell for some interviews. He needed help in his firm and I guess he wanted somebody cheap who could do accurate work. Help doesn't come any cheaper than a new graduate."

"You stuck with him for over twenty years. That's impressive loyalty," said Stan.

"When I think back on it now, I realize he wanted someone to play on his bridge team as much as he needed help in his company. He liked to play with Ted Lugner regularly, and he wanted someone willing to play with Louise. It didn't take much persuasion to get me to come along to tournaments with them. He was my boss, after all. I enjoyed tournaments a lot anyway."

"You must have had some qualifications that interested him."

"I was never a great student, but I did well in a finance course — top of the class — the only one I did really well in. I love bonds. Theory, practicalities, you name it. I talked to Harry about bond market details, but I don't think he really ever understood what I was saying. What Harry really liked was that I was a keen bridge player. We played bridge that first night at the university club and I think I impressed him."

"And you wanted to come to a small place like Erieville?"

"In my last year of college, I was one of the guys without even one job offer. I wasn't sure I'd get one. I can tell you I was pretty excited when he came up with what I thought was a pretty generous proposition. I was ready to accept on the spot."

"What exactly do you do here?" Stan looked around the room.

"I recommend investments to our clients. Really, my specialty over the years has been bonds. They've cooled off a lot recently. When I first started, interest rates were at an all-time high. It didn't take a genius to make a fortune. You just had to be in the business and know your way around. Interest rates were running fifteen percent for a while. Half a brain would tell you rates were going to come down. That's when bonds go up."

"Can you do better than buying municipal bonds and sitting on them?"

"They're certainly safe. And you get a tax deduction. I like high yield bonds, but you have to watch out for defaults. Every now and then you get a really bad year. Last year was the worst since I've been in the business. I mean ten percent default. We had a couple of bad years in '90 and '91. Other than that, we've done all right."

Stan nodded. He was quickly losing interest.

"The most volatile bond segments are less erratic than the most stable stock market segments. Even if you have three or four percent defaults in your portfolio some years, you can still make money. You won't have that level of default every year, either. Moody's or Standard and Poor always give you a pretty good forecast of bond default rates. Of course, you have to apply your own judgment to it. When the economy goes sour, default rates can go way up. But often, you can see it coming. The other thing you want to do is diversify. Taking a small piece of a hundred bonds is less risky than bigger pieces of ten, and tiny bits of five hundred are better than small pieces of one hundred. It's possible to pick a good portfolio and adjust from time to time. You can certainly beat the rates on government bonds, by a good margin."

"I didn't follow any of that," said Stan.

"Most people don't, but once you get the hang of it, it's pretty simple."

Stan was surprised by how alive and animated Johnson appeared when he talked about bonds. *He's probably like that when he gets going on bridge, too*, he thought.

"How did Lache manage to leave his business to you?"

"We were pretty good friends. The business was in Louise's name, you know. Not Harry's. She put all the money into it. She made a note in her will that I would take over if something happened to them both. I'm not sure that Harry even knew about it. He sure as hell didn't care. He lived one day at a time. Drank, smoked, screwed around like crazy. Your ultimate hedonist."

"And he made buckets of money in his little business here?"

"I made all his money for him. Look, I'm a realist. I took advantage of the opportunity that was there. I've done the square root since. Five or six percent a year, maybe. That's all. But in the early eighties, we had a bonanza. There are guys who make thirty percent on bonds even now. Some of the fellows running the bond segment of endowment funds would bowl you over. They're utter geniuses, like Rodwell at the bridge table. I'm not that good."

"How did you get Mrs. Lache to sign over the business to you?"

Johnson reddened at this. "Like I said, we were very good friends. Very close. We were on a streak one year where we won every tournament in sight. We even managed to win one national championship. We were lucky, but I'll take it. Louise and I got pretty chummy that year. She would have done anything for me. So I suggested, just in case anything happened to them, that I would need to look after my interests. The Laches were fifteen years older than I am. She went along right away."

"And you benefited greatly from their deaths," urged Stan.

Johnson hesitated at this suggestive remark. "Obviously I did. Only a fool would see it differently. I can see your mind churning over motive. Well, I'm not your man. I hope I don't need to hire a lawyer to convince you."

"Not at this point, certainly. We can't rule anybody in or out. If you're innocent, you have nothing to worry about."

Stan found Beth to be a much more interesting study. She had the polite manner of a person used to pleasing customers, and he found this at odds with her perpetually serious look. She responded to all of his questions, but nothing he said would induce as much as a twitch of a smile to the corners of her lips.

"You've been in this business a while," began Stan.

"Twenty-seven years now. I started when I was nineteen. Harry was great to work for, and Ron and I get along fine."

"You've been here longer than your friend?" Stan asked, nodding in Johnson's direction.

"He's been here over twenty years. He's a genius with bonds. He's made a ton of money for our customers. I do the actual trading, but he tells me what issues to buy and how much. We get into a million dollars a trade some times."

"You do a lot of trading?"

"Well, no. Not really. We buy these bonds and when some of them come due or when Ron gets some news, he asks me to trade them. When I say trade, I just buy and sell what Ron asks. I don't go off on my own and sell stuff. And we only have a few customers. Ten or eleven altogether, that's all. I mean, we have some small accounts from people around town. But Harry had these old friends of his. I guess they went back a long way. He had their accounts. Then when Ron joined us, it wasn't too long after that that the bond market seemed to take off. At least the issues that Ron recommended. A few of the companies defaulted, but everyone made money in spite of that."

"He sounds like a guy I should talk to about my finances."

"He'd be glad to."

"So Ron owns the firm now?"

Beth nodded.

"Did the Laches have any children?"

"No. Louise had a niece. Ron contacted her and she came to town after the disappearances. After the Laches had been missing for three years, they were declared legally dead. That's the law in New York. She set the wheels in motion for the death notice. The niece got all of Louise's money and the two houses. The big one here in town and the one on Wellesley Island. Louise came from money. She bankrolled Harry in his business, but they left the firm to Ron. He took over everything. Ron has a copy of a document that gave him title to the whole business in the event that she and Harry died."

"You and Ron run the whole business by yourselves? Just the two of you?"

"We have a clerk to do filing and typing. She comes in three days a week. But apart from that, Ron and I handle it all. Harry had these friends who were his customers. All he ever did was play golf and bridge with them. Ron is the guy who made all the money for the clients. We had four or five customers while Harry was alive. They're all millionaires and a small percentage fee from their investments is a decent income for Ron and me. We've added a few clients since then, and one of Harry's friends has died. We're doing okay."

"Did Louise or Harry leave you anything in the will?"

"Not much. I got a package of a few thousand dollars. Ron is the guy who really benefited, apart from the niece, I mean."

Stan became awkward. He knew the interview was concluding and he would have to leave. He desperately searched for some fine words, some way to make a big impression that would lead to further time in Beth's company. Nothing came to him, and he reluctantly settled for an inane departing remark.

"Thanks for your help," he said. "I'll be around town for a few days."

"My pleasure, Stan. I'm not busy in the evenings, if you need anything."

He could hardly believe his ears; his adrenaline took another surge. Searching his mind for an excuse to stay in Erieville for the evening, he realized that involvement with a possible witness, or indeed, a suspect, would be at odds with his position as an investigating officer in the case. *On the other hand*, he thought, *a little time with Beth might be worth it.*

"I'll take down your number, if you don't mind. I'll have some more questions when we're a little further along."

When he had gone as far as he could probing details of Lache's car, Fraser called the number he had for Ted Lugner. The phone rang several times and finally an elderly, out-of-breath voice answered, "Lugner."

Fraser introduced himself and explained the nature of his visit. Lugner invited him to "Come on over anytime."

Fraser found that the Lugner residence was a few blocks from the Laches' former home in another of Erieville's giant, ancient wooden-frame houses, built in the nineteenth century when the costs of building and heating the huge rambling structures were a tiny fraction of present values. He noted that the yard was well maintained with trimmed lawns, stately oak and maple trees over one hundred feet high showing spring buds, and healthy looking beds of perennials poking through the ground. As he parked, he could hear the crashing blows of an axe from the backyard. When he walked around to the back, he spotted a tall, perspiring, silver-haired gentleman and a lithe young fellow working on a pile of firewood. Fraser watched the pair for a moment before walking up to introduce himself.

The older man was swinging a good sized axe in a great arc, driving it hard enough to bite into the reluctant wood, then taking a small sledge to hammer it through. When he ultimately succeeded in parting a log, he set up each half and repeated the process. The youth moved the split wood into the back door of Lugner's huge three-car garage.

"Hello there," Fraser called.

The older man nodded, lumbered over and the two introduced themselves. A quick handshake proved that the older man retained a great deal of his strength even in his declining years. The youngster interrupted his work briefly to look over at Fraser, scowled, but did not speak.

"I see you cut your own firewood," said Fraser.

"These old white oaks are tough as hell right now. They're easier to split when they're frozen solid, but I can't wait for winter. You finally get the axe into them, and think you've got a piece split, but the fibers still hang together in spots and you have to bang the axe all the way through."

"You could keep busy with this pile for quite a while," said Fraser.

"Yes," said Lugner. "Look at all these old trees on the lot. Sadly, one has to come down every now and then. This baby must be a hundred-and-fifty years old, at least. They keep me supplied. I need help taking them down, but Jason here helps me and we can handle the rest of the job ourselves. Good exercise. I chop it all and, as a matter of fact, I saw it myself. I hate those new-fangled chain saws. A friend of mine ripped his hand almost all the way off. You have to watch every second with those things. I still know how to sharpen a saw so it cuts like a razor. How about a drink?"

Fraser turned down offers of scotch and bourbon and accepted coffee. Lugner led him into the back door of his house. A walnut-paneled hallway led to a large study, which was furnished with old but still beautiful oriental rugs and leather furniture.

Lugner disappeared into his kitchen and Fraser took a seat in a comfortable, overstuffed chair. He was pleased to note that his difficulty sitting had almost disappeared over the past few days. As he looked around, he heard a rustle and saw a furry animal streak across the rug. The animal found a spot in a bookcase and peered down at him with large round eyes. As Fraser got up to look closely at the bookcase, the creature leapt away and scampered out of the room. *It's awfully big for a mouse,* he thought. *Mice don't like daylight. Does he have rats here?*

Lugner returned and Fraser was still looking intently at the bookcase. "You seem to have some animal life here," said Fraser.

Lugner chuckled. "That's Jason's ferret. My old dog died a couple of years ago. He used to keep him out of trouble, but these days he gets into everything. He doesn't hurt anything."

Lugner handed him a mug and sat down in the couch across from him.

"So you're looking into the Lache mystery. Harry and Louise," said Lugner. "It's been a while now."

"Four years, give or take."

"You're from Genessee county, you said on the phone. How did you come to be assigned to this case? I thought state police pretty much worked within their own counties."

"We usually do," answered Fraser. "In this case, the two victims were bridge players. Gordon Bryder, my boss in Buffalo, figured that someone with a connection to the universe of bridge might have a better chance of sorting out this mess."

"Were you involved in the Buffalo case a couple of years ago? Smithers and poor old Hermann?"

"I headed up the investigation team."

"That was well done. You're a pretty good bridge player yourself then?"

"I like to think so. I've won a few regionals, but I have no illusions about my shortcomings. You were good friends with the Laches, I take it?" asked Fraser.

"Oh yes," said Lugner, smiling. "Forty years maybe. Let me see. I was at Louise and Harry's wedding. They were married in 1958."

"Good friends all that time?"

"The best. We played bridge for years. Harry was my best partner and Louise was always on our team."

"Do you have any idea as to who had it in for them?"

"That's an interesting question. Damned interesting. I've wondered about Harry and Louise for the past four years. Wondered what in heaven happened to them. They disappeared without saying goodbye. I always figured something bad happened, and I told the guy, Cameron, my feelings. Nobody had any proof or any hard evidence until the bodies turned up."

"You must have some theory," encouraged Fraser.

"I hate to talk about it. You get a theory and if you talk about it, it means pointing a finger at someone."

"This is murder, of course, and we can't let personal feelings stand in the way of getting at facts."

"No. No. I understand where you're coming from. I still hate to talk about it. It puzzles the dickens out of me how this guy Ron Johnson got hold of Harry's

company. Harry had his investment company here in Erieville — very small pota-
toes — but a few of us did very well sticking with him. Actually, sticking with
Johnson is a better way to put it. He has a gift with bonds. I mucked around for
years making three or four percent, but this guy knows bonds. He saw all the
spikes coming in the last twenty years, and if you were a client, you rode on his
wings. A few years I earned twenty-five percent, had a few in the high teens, hardly ever dropped below ten percent. That's all changed in the past few years. I've
hardly made anything the past four years, but who cares. I'm set for life — the few
years I've got left."

"So what about Johnson and the Laches?"

"The part that I wonder about is that Johnson got the whole thing when they
were declared dead. The whole business, I mean. When the Laches disappeared,
they weren't legally dead until they had been gone for three years. The business
was in Louise's name. Harry didn't have a pot to piss in when they were married.
Louise set him up with an office and he got a few friends to switch their business
to him, myself included. We coasted along for several years, and then he hired
Johnson right out of school. Johnson was a bridge nut at school — that's what
caught Harry's interest. The guy has no personality. He couldn't give a bond to a
beggar. But man, does he know his technical stuff.

"I never figured out how he got the business. Louise must have signed it over
to him somewhere along the way. In her will, I mean. The Laches had no kids and
Louise's niece got the balance. She didn't need it, either. She had more money than
Louise."

"Interesting. So Johnson got the whole business?"

"The office, furniture, computers. The company owned everything. They
didn't believe in leasing. Didn't have to. And of course, the customers came with
the business. But Johnson would have gotten them anyway. Everybody recognized
that he was the brains behind the business. Harry would never admit that."

"And Louise never mentioned this to anyone?"

"Not to me. I always wondered how close she and Johnson were. They played
a lot of bridge together. Harry was not exactly a model of the faithful husband. He
wandered quite a bit. I'm sure Louise knew about it. She and Ron may have had
a thing going. The more I thought about it over the past few years, the more I con-
vinced myself that must be what happened."

"Johnson had a lot to gain if the Laches left the scene."

"That's what's on my mind," said Lugner. "I've always wondered if there was a connection somewhere. Louise was turning a little cool towards Johnson the last few times they were together. I never liked Johnson personally, but what a great mind. Terrific bond man and a great bridge player as well. We won a lot of tournaments — wouldn't have done it without him. He was a much stronger player than Louise. Stronger than Harry, too."

Fraser noted that Lugner did not compare Johnson to himself. He took another sip of coffee.

"So you're saying that Johnson had a thing going with Louise for a while. They got close and he put her up to leaving him the business. Then the relationship cools and he thinks he'd better get busy."

"I hate to say it. You asked me about a theory. What can an old man do when his best friends disappear?"

"No one else comes to mind as having a grudge against the two of them?"

"The girl in the office there, Beth. She isn't exactly rich and neither is she beautiful. Always seemed to do a good job for the Laches, though. She may have tried to get sweet with Johnson, but that never went anywhere. Maybe he was never interested, or maybe Louise's presence was all Johnson could handle. The two of them have stuck it out in the business, though. You might think they were together on whatever happened, but I don't think Beth got any of the business. She just kept her job. That was probably all she wanted."

Fraser set his cup down on the sideboard and stood up.

"Okay. Thanks. I'll be leaving now. We'll be around this area for a while and I'll be back at some point to go over things."

"If you're in town for a while, you ought to come out to our local club one night. The bridge is nothing special — same as clubs the world over — but you'd have a chance to meet all the locals and maybe pick up a lead or two."

"I'll think about it," said Fraser.

"I wouldn't mind a game if you're interested. We have a game Thursdays at seven that's as good as any."

"I could handle that. Gossip is one of the best sources for clues in any case. The trail here is so cold that I'll need everything I can get."

"Thursday it is," said Lugner, and Fraser took his leave.

CHAPTER 5

On Wednesday evening, shortly after six, Fraser invited his fellow officers to gather in his hotel room in the Wellesley Island motel. They had indicated interest in bourbon and Budweiser, duly provided, while he satisfied himself with lukewarm tea. Stan was the first to arrive. He carefully measured a moderate aliquot of whisky into a plastic glass and added exactly two ice cubes. Macvey joined them shortly after and attacked the beer with gusto, using one bottle as an opener to snap caps off another.

"What happened to you?" Fraser asked of Macvey, noting the readily visible facial cuts and awkward repairs.

"I ran into some turkeys," mumbled Macvey. "They surprised the hell out of me. I never saw those buggers before. They're vicious. One jumped in the car through the sun roof. I should never have had the damned thing open."

"How about your shoulder?" asked Fraser. "Looks like somebody smashed it up too."

"I came across this woman, Lucy. Lucy Dinde. She could have been a professional wrestler. Tried to whack me with her shovel."

"Looks like she succeeded," said Stan, smirking. "What else did your new friend do for you?"

"Aw, she just bruised my shoulder a bit. She gave me a coffee and cookies later. She didn't mean anything. I must have surprised her. Those people don't see many visitors. She's one strong babe. She could have planted both the Laches in that spot."

"What motive would she have?" asked Fraser.

"Hard to say from a short talk. She says she knew the couple pretty well. Used to drop in and play bridge with them now and then. Got totally pissed off one day when they took a bunch of money off her. She swears that Lache and this guy Lugner were cheating. The whole thing was very friendly and nice, but she says there was all kinds of table talk between them during the game. Anyway, they fleeced her this one night and she quit going over."

"That's hardly a reason to kill someone," said Fraser. "Bridge games aren't usually very high stakes games. Not like poker. You get a couple of hundred dollars changing hands in a game, that's all. Did she say how much she lost?"

"She said a thousand dollars. That'd be enough to set me back."

Stan whistled. "Some game."

"What about the other neighbors?" asked Fraser. "You drew a blank there?"

"Only one guy at home. His name is Dan Gehl. An old bugger. Handyman. He says Lache was humping the Dinde lady. They went at it for the good part of a year. Then something happened and they quit seeing each other. This old guy says he used to do some work for the Laches. He spoke well of them."

"Anybody else?" asked Fraser.

"Nobody else at home. Lucy says the Hills are due back this weekend. Evidently they were really good friends with the Laches. Sounds like they'd be worth talking to. Lucy mentioned that the old guy, Gehl, looked like he was taking furniture out of the Lache place one day and moving it into his own. Maybe he had an arrangement. Maybe he was stealing. Anyhow, she saw him carting stuff away."

"And he lives here year round?"

"Yeah. Lucy and Gehl both. Most of the others come here just for the summers. Some come for a bit of winter activity. But those two are the only ones around there that live full-time on the island."

Fraser turned to the other man.

"How was your day, Stan?"

Stan produced his notebook and reviewed its contents. "I visited Lache's old office and talked to a Ron Johnson and a Beth Harper."

"Those names are becoming familiar," observed Fraser.

"You heard of them, too?" asked Stan. "Johnson runs the business now. He's a creep. Beth works for him. She seems like a genuine lady. She has real presence. And she has a grip like one of those Amazons."

"You like this lady," suggested Fraser.

Stan reddened but didn't lose his composure. He continued. "They knew the Laches well, of course. The most important item I turned up was that the guy in the office seems to have had the most to gain by getting rid of the Laches. He took over the whole business. He became a rich man when they died."

"A bit early for theories, isn't it?"

"I was just giving you facts," bristled Stan.

"Along with color commentary," added Brad.

"But you're right. We have to start somewhere," continued Fraser. "Suppose someone was after the Laches' money. They knew the Laches were driving to San Antonio for a big bridge tournament. They knew all the dates and travel times. They interrupted their trip somehow or other, killed the couple, brought their bodies up here, buried them one night and disposed of the car later."

"How can you dispose of a car?" asked Brad. "The things don't just evaporate."

"About a million cars evaporate every year in the US. Thousands in New York state alone. They disappear and are never seen again. It's no trick to find a ring that buys cars at a fraction of their value. That was my job before I got into the criminal investigation branch."

"What, buying hot cars?" wondered Brad.

Fraser ignored him. "Most of them are stripped down and sold for parts. They end up in Mexico, Europe, Asia. A few are just repainted and sold here in the States. They file off original serial numbers and engrave new ones."

"We might have a hope if the car is still in the States," said Stan. "Otherwise, we can forget it."

"Exactly," agreed Fraser. "Anyway, I dropped in on the dealer and got the original serial numbers and complete specs. I talked to a couple of my old contacts in the stolen car business. The guy in Buffalo suggests maybe somewhere in the South as a place to start looking."

"That narrows it down to maybe a hundred million square miles," drawled Stan.

"He's thinking close to the gulf. I talked to Mike Eppler in Albany. You know him? He's number one in tracking stolen vehicles, right across the country. I asked him to see if they can help us find the Cadillac."

"Fine," said Stan. "On a cold case like this, you got to grasp at straws."

Fraser summarized his talk with Ted Lugner and then the officers went to the hotel dining room. They laid plans for the next day as they ordered and consumed their meal.

"You say this couple, the Hills, are due back this weekend?" asked Fraser.

"That's what Lucy said," affirmed Macvey. "Can we believe her? I don't know."

"Somebody should be around to talk to them," suggested Stan.

"Somebody might want to talk to Beth this weekend, too," said Fraser, laughing.

Macvey let it be known that he was not at all interested in staying in the vicinity over the weekend. "My girlfriend's birthday. I gave her my solemn word I'd take her out."

"She'll understand if you tell her you're on an important case," said Stan.

"Don't tell me you guys are both working the whole weekend," said Brad.

"I just volunteered. I'm sure Captain Fraser has important things to look into here. We can't just drop the case."

"Yeah, but I promised," said Brad.

"Doesn't she understand police work?"

Fraser thought the kidding had gone on far enough. "Listen, I have to go to Buffalo for some personal business myself. I can get back here late on Sunday. Stan can check out the Hills if he wants. That would be useful."

"I can check into some other things as well. Nose around the neighbors. I have nothing on my plate."

"And you get paid by the hour," said Brad.

The others ignored this. "I've been all alone since my wife left me," said Stan with a shrug.

"I'm sorry to hear that," said Fraser. "I didn't know."

"I'm not sorry she left. She drinks like a fish and she'll talk your head off if you let her. Never stops. I have to hand out support payments every month, but I get by. This contract work is a godsend. The last straw was a trip to Paris. Wonderful idea, I thought. We had a great fight over it. Our hotel was okay, but it wasn't top line. She complained about that. She complained about the subway. She complained about the shit on the streets. I mean Paris is a dump in a lot of respects, but it's also supposed to be the city of lovers, you know? I thought I was doing her a big favor. Anyway, I got robbed and she hardly noticed. We're walking down the street, she's talking a blue streak, and this guy comes up and puts a knife to me. I couldn't do a damned thing. He asks for my wallet, and he and his partner take all my cash. She doesn't even know what's happening — she's so engrossed in complaining. At least I got my wallet back. They threw it on the ground and ran off." He stared into space for a moment before shrugging again. "You don't have that problem, I guess," he said to Fraser.

"No. Still a bachelor. I'm staying that way for the time being."

"I hear you have a couple of friends you live with," said Brad. "You've got to teach me your system."

Macvey's last question made Fraser begin to feel uncomfortable. He had watched the pair put away a decent amount of liquor in the last few hours, which accounted for their loosened tongues, but it still felt a bit intense, especially considering the changed situation with Karen and Jill.

"Not much to teach," responded Fraser. "We're just friends from a long way back. One of them is moving out this month. Thinks I fart too much. Wanted me to stop eating beans." Stan and Brad roared at this.

"Look," continued Fraser, eager to change the subject. "We don't want to make this investigation a long-term career stop. We've got to get moving. Brad, maybe you can take us around to meet your Lucy tomorrow morning. Then we can go down to Erieville right after and cross check the stories from Lugner and the two at Lache's old company. Any other ideas how to go about it?"

"Whatever you say, long as I'm in Syracuse for Saturday night," said Brad.

"Somebody should get in touch with the niece," said Stan.

Fraser nodded agreement. "We ought to get her up here as soon as possible and see what she knows. I'll look after contacting her," he said. "Do you think we need to talk to more of the neighbors in Erieville?"

"If you want to," said Brad. "I told you my experience. The murder happened a long time ago. There's hardly anybody around from four years ago. Those who are around have forgotten everything by now."

"Okay," said Fraser. "Cameron says he'll have someone do clerical stuff for us. Make up a list of acquaintances. Whoever is free can start with some of the calls. Stan, if you're staying the weekend, you might as well get that organized."

Stan grunted assent.

"I need to have a personal chat with Johnson and Beth. Sounds like the woman will be more helpful than the man. I should talk to her first. What time do they start work at the office in Erieville?" he asked Stan.

"Usually at nine. The office isn't busy and it's a very informal setup. There are only three people working there — Johnson, Beth, and a part-time secretary. Wouldn't surprise me if they got in late occasionally. I had a pretty good chat with both of them, Naturally, if you don't trust my report, you and Brad had better get over there and see for yourself."

"This has nothing to do with trust, Stan. The murder happened a long time ago. People sometimes remember in stages, not all at once. Talking about it sometimes brings other memories back to mind. Maybe the two of us could run over the facts you dug up yesterday. We have to go over all the testimony several times. With key witnesses, you never know what might be important."

"I was going to talk to her again myself for that very reason," said Stan. "We don't want to upset the lady. Not at this point, anyway. She's been damned cooperative."

Fraser let the matter go at that. He sensed that Stan agreed with him on the matter of police procedure, but had a more personal reason for wanting to stay on the right side of Beth. This might lead to a problem if matters went a certain way. Fraser made a mental note to keep an eye on the situation.

CHAPTER 6

On Thursday morning, the three officers arrived within minutes of one another in the breakfast room of the Wellesley Island motel. Predictably, Stan was early, Brad was late, and Art was right on time. Coffee was good; bacon, eggs, waffles, pancakes and cereal were all plentiful. Macvey savored the bacon and eggs, along with the waffles and pancakes. His serving of toast turned out to be an unappetizing fragment of charcoal. "Miss?" he called to the server.

"What's that, honey?" she asked.

"I'm not fussy about black. Does this come in grey?" he said, pointing to the toast.

The woman inspected the condition of the serving, picked up plate and toast, and in one fluid move, wheeled on one toe and jettisoned the black residue into a nearby waste container. She made her way to the kitchen with the empty dish, kicked one of the swinging doors briskly, and called out, "One order of wheat toast, rare."

"Are we lined up to see your friend Lucy?" asked Fraser.

"She says don't come too early."

"Meaning?"

"I never asked."

"Well, I guess we can go somewhere else first. What do you suggest?"

"You're the boss, but I say visit old Gehl. He gets up pretty early from Lucy's account. He knows more than he's talked about so far."

"How long will he take?"

"We could stretch it out for a couple of hours maybe. See Lucy about ten."

"That'll waste the whole morning," complained Stan.

Fraser said, "Maybe not waste. We don't have a hell of a lot to go on yet. Somebody has to know something. Maybe Gehl does."

"I never talked to him about a follow up," said Brad.

"Something's gotta give," said Stan. "We can't spend all spring up here waiting for appointments. Let's go see them. Get them the hell out of bed and talk to them."

"Hold on now," said Fraser. "We don't need to turn any of these folks against us. Let's take one step at a time. Okay. Gehl first. Then we go see Lucy. Then we spend the afternoon in Erieville, all three of us, talking to the key witnesses we have there."

"Fine," said Stan. "And I stay around for the weekend and talk to Erieville neighbors, if I can find any. And we get together Monday morning. I might as well check into a motel in Erieville for the weekend. I don't see any point in staying around here."

"That sounds fair," said Fraser. "Off we go."

The detectives checked out of the Wellesley Island motel and took their separate cars to the vicinity of the Lache property. Macvey led them to Gehl's home. The dogs ran out to greet them, barking ferociously. Brad laughed at Stan's quick, uncomfortable moves to sidestep them. A few whistled notes drew the pack towards him and then Brad wrestled and cavorted physically with each of the dogs in turn, leaving a clear path to the door for his colleagues. Gehl answered the door shirtless, in rumpled trousers, bright suspenders contrasting with grayish underwear. A cigarette dangled from his lips.

"What'n hell you guys want?" he snarled. "I gave the big guy everything he asked for." When he noticed Macvey in the background, his attitude softened. "Oh hi, Brad. Didn't see you."

"Hi, Dan," said Macvey, who stepped over the dogs to introduce his colleagues. "We need a lot more information. We'll be back a few more times before you see the last of us."

"Might as well come in then. I can make a fresh pot. Find yourselves a chair, such as they are."

The kitchen furniture looked strangely out of place in the dingy surroundings. A decent quality maple kitchen set with leather upholstered chairs clashed with dirty vinyl flooring and a sink full of dishes.

"We're close to pinning down the exact date of the Lache murders," said Fraser. "We believe it was July 19, 1999, give or take a couple of days. We're hoping you may remember something happening around that time. You're here year round, aren't you?"

"Yeah. No place else to go. I like it here, winter or summer. They stopped coming up here some time that summer. Bang. Just like that. So it was '99, eh?

Man, time flies. It's coming back a bit now. It all seemed so funny. They were here in June and early July, then all of a sudden I didn't see them any more. Never again. He owed me some money, too. I looked after the grounds and did a few odd jobs for them. I kept it up all summer, right up until frost. Then I quit. They never came back up after July. I helped myself to this kitchen set here. Figured Harry wouldn't mind. He was a fair man to deal with. Always threw in a tip. I sure miss him."

"Can you see their lot from here?" asked Stan, looking around the room with distaste.

"Look out that window," said Gehl, pointing to a streaked pane of glass. "This time of year, when the leaves are just busting out, you can see the whole property. In the summer, you can't see far at all. 'Course, the trees have thickened up a bit since '99, but even then you couldn't see far in the summer."

"Do you remember anything strange happening during that summer, right around the time they stopped coming up here? Maybe in the middle of the night, or any time at all?" asked Fraser.

"I can't say as I really saw anything special in daytime. At night, well I don't recall anything right now. Maybe it'll come to me. Sound travels pretty good here, especially at night when all you got is the animals. I hear most everything going on, until I go to bed, anyway. I turn in about ten every night. This is a pretty quiet place."

Fraser asked, "Did you talk to anyone else about the Laches' disappearance?"

"We all talk," said Gehl. "I talked to Lucy down the street. She noticed they weren't coming. She said she wasn't sorry if she never saw them again. Then there's the Hills. They knew the Laches better'n any of us."

"Where's their house?" asked Stan, holding his notebook at the ready.

"Across the road and down a quarter mile. On the left."

"Were they here at the time Laches disappeared?"

"They were here all right. Oh, maybe they got here right after."

"Did they make any comments about the disappearance?"

"Hill said something to me. I can't remember exactly what now. Lemme think. He may have noticed something. They'll be up this month. They're usually here early in spring for a week or so. Matter of fact, I wouldn't be surprised if they're here this weekend. Lucy'd know. You ought to ask her."

"Do you know where the Hill's permanent home is?" asked Fraser.

"Their home is in Allentown, Pennsylvania or near there. But I don't know the address. Lucy might. She gets into all that stuff. I mind my own business, pretty much. I'll tell you this, though. Nobody liked the Hills very much. Neither him nor her."

"Why's that?" asked Stan.

"Well, first of all, he's an arse. I mean, a tightwad. Never pays willingly. You do a job and you have to coax every cent out of him to get paid. Not like Harry. Harry always had a tip, and he come over asking how much he owed."

"And Mrs. Hill?" asked Macvey.

"She's kind of a good looker. I never trusted her. She'd be maybe fifty, fifty-five. Trying to pass herself off as thirty. Keeps herself slim. Always wears tight clothes. Nice tits. Smiles like a phony. I never liked her. Never will. Lucy never liked them either."

"Do you work for them?" asked Fraser.

"Did is more like it," said Gehl. "Never again. Collecting from that sonofabitch is something else. Too painful for yours truly."

"And you think they'll be back here soon?" asked Piper.

"Could be this weekend. They usually come up every year for a spring cleanup."

Stan thanked Gehl for the coffee and the officers left to go to Lucy's place.

"What did you make of all that?" asked Fraser when they were well away from the house.

Brad frowned. "His story was a little different than when I talked to him last time."

"How so?"

"He didn't bad mouth the Hills like he did just now. And he seems to be a lot closer to Lucy than he let on before. When he said 'Lucy never liked them either', it sounded like he and Lucy are thick."

"That's the impression I got too," said Stan. "They're sure as hell good neighborhood friends."

They reached Lucy Dinde's house shortly before ten and saw a vigorous form attacking leaves and other debris with a rake. Macvey shouted hello as he left his car and walked toward her.

"What do you want?" she demanded.

"I brought my friends along. They want to meet you. Besides, I figure I need a bodyguard when I come over here."

"Friends, huh?"

Fraser stepped forward. "We need more information on the Laches. We're hoping you'll help us."

"Bunch of slickers like you, I thought you'd have this all figured out by now. Come on into the kitchen. I'll make some coffee and I'll tell you all I know. How's your shoulder, honey?"

Brad reddened at the familiarity. "Not a problem," he lied.

For the second time that morning, the trio sat around a domestic kitchen drinking strong coffee, this time with Lucy's admirable oatmeal cookies. Her huge kitchen was scrubbed clean. Tasteful decorations in yellow and gray, with a chrome-trimmed kitchen table and a worn leather rocking chair in front of a large TV gave a homey impression. This was a welcome change from the place Gehl kept.

"As far as we can tell," said Fraser, "the Laches were brought up here the night of July 19, 1999. They may have been alive when they got here, but we believe they were buried on their lot on about that date. Just try and think back four years. We need to piece together what happened around that time. Do you remember anything special going on around then? We realize you may not be able to tell us much today, but maybe we can jog your memory."

"I remember that time all right," said Lucy. "It seemed strange that those people seemed to come here regularly and then all of a sudden they stopped coming. Their place was kept up that year. I guess Dan did that for them. Dan Gehl, I mean. But everything was so quiet."

"Someone must have come up here in the middle of the night and dragged two bodies on to the lot, dug a hole and buried them," continued Fraser. "That would make a lot of noise, and someone might have heard the car or seen the headlights in the dark."

"Can you see the Lache place from here, Mrs. Dinde?" Stan asked.

"It's right across the road. You can see it easy from the front of my house. See for yourself. You can't see anything out front from the kitchen. This is where I spend most of my time."

"If you think back to that summer, do you have a diary or any notes that might help you remember what went on?" pursued Fraser.

"I never kept a diary. Nothing comes to mind right now. I told Brad that I wasn't on good terms with the Laches after they screwed me out of a bunch of money in a bridge game. I still liked Louise, but that no-good husband of hers gave me the creeps. So I wasn't keeping track of them at all that summer."

"We'll come back to that later," said Fraser. "You know the Hills?"

"Sure. Thank goodness for them. The only sane people up here, except for Dan. I hardly ever see them, but they're decent. They kept on being friends with the Laches even after I told them what happened. I expect they'll be here soon. They generally show up in the spring to clean up and get ready for the season."

"Were they around during that time in '99?" asked Stan. "The time when the Laches may have been buried?"

"I think they were. Yes. Must have been. They were here the last half of July. They may have seen something or heard something."

"Do you have their address? We need to get in touch with them. If they're coming here, we should arrange to meet them. Otherwise, we'll have to go to Allentown."

"I have it somewhere," said Lucy. She gave the officers a copy of the Hill's address and a phone number in Allentown, and they said goodbye, promising to drop in again the following week.

"I'll be here," she said.

The officers paraded out, with Macvey bringing up the rear, a cookie in each large hand. He flinched as Lucy grabbed his tender shoulder and said, "Don't forget, Brad, anytime you feel like coming over and wiggling some stumps out for me, you're more than welcome."

The officers drove to Erieville individually. Fraser met Macvey at the car rental agency where the latter dropped off his vehicle.

"Cameron's going to love me for this," said Brad.

"He gives you a hard time, does he?" asked Fraser.

"You'd think it was his own money, the way he goes over every expense account I send in. A senior man like him shouldn't have time to worry about nickels."

"A thousand dollars makes a lot of nickels."

"True, but it's all in the line of duty."

They went on to join Stan at a restaurant near the Lache office.

"They're expecting us at one o'clock," said Stan. "Both Beth and Johnson will be in."

"Fine. Any ideas on how we should arrange these interviews?"

"If we do it like we did Gehl and Lucy, we'll be more confused when we finish," said Macvey.

"Why?"

"Gehl says Lucy disliked the Hills. She says she liked them. That's a little screwy if you ask me."

"It's strange," agreed Fraser. "I'm not sure what to make of it. That's why we go at these people a couple of times — get rid of some of the discrepancies. Everybody claims to be innocent. When we spot contrary stories, we start to make a little progress. With Beth and Johnson, we just go over the same ground Stan did. Only this time Brad and I ask the questions. We've got to find something we can latch on to."

At one o'clock sharp, Stan introduced his fellow officers to Beth and Ron. They chatted for a few minutes while Beth served them coffee, and then Stan stepped up to take charge. "We'd like to talk to each of you singly and together. I'll be taking notes. Eventually we'll want you to sign a statement for us."

Fraser glared at Stan. The man was certainly overstepping his place, but he decided this was not a time to make an issue of it. *Stan is trying to make an impression on the lady*, he thought.

"You can use my office for a couple of hours if you want," said Johnson. "I have a couple of errands to do in the meantime."

The officers were surprised at this offer, but glad to accept it. Johnson's office took up over half the space that the firm occupied. The chairs were comfortable and furniture was impressive. A picture of Harry Lache glowered down from behind Johnson's desk. A smaller, but infinitely kinder picture of Louise looked over matters from another wall.

"Why don't you sit in the boss's chair, Beth?" asked Stan.

Fraser glared once again, but let matters ride. The three detectives sat around the massive desk and focused on Beth. "Well, gentlemen," she said grimly. "Let's bring this meeting to order."

"I second the motion," said Stan.

"I thought you were taking notes," said Fraser. He turned to address Beth. "We need to go over everything you can think of related to the murder. Any event you can recall from around that time might help us. We believe that Harry and Louise were last seen during the day of July 19, 1999. That was a Monday. They were planning to drive to San Antonio to play in a bridge tournament. Ron was going to join them on Thursday, July 22. Can you fill in any events from that time? Before or after the specific date?"

"Let me get my calendar book," said Beth. "It's not a diary, but I do have all our appointments in it. I can remember Mr. Lache's plan to take two weeks off. Some other things may come back. Just give me a minute."

Beth returned shortly with a large binder and thumbed through it to a place that seemed of interest. "Here we are. July 9. Sold some bonds for Mr. Lugner. July 11 — meeting at the golf course. They had a meeting there every Wednesday. They were up at Wellesley the week before that. I made hotel reservations for him and Mrs. Lache, and I made a note of the phone number where I could reach him. Ron and I pretty much ran the office when Mr. Lache was away."

Fraser asked, "So the last time you saw Lache was on Friday, July 16?"

"According to my calendar I gave him an itinerary for his trip. He had hotel reservations along the way. I gave him his confirmation number for that and the one in San Antonio. Same thing for the trip home — same place. A Hilton in Nashville, Tennessee."

"When was the last time you saw Mrs. Lache?"

"Oh, that's hard to say. I think she dropped in when Mr. Lache was at his meeting, golf meeting that is."

"On the Wednesday afternoon?"

"Yes, that was it. She often did that. She and Ron had a lot to talk about. They'd come into this office, close the door, and talk for the longest time. Sometimes they'd go out together for an hour or two."

"What did they do? And talk about? Any idea?"

"Not really. I'm not nosy by nature. I know one thing, though. They talked about bridge a lot. They played a lot together. I'm not a player, but I guess you have to talk over your system and things to be really good."

"Did they get along well together?"

"You'd have to ask them. I'm not big on gossip."

Fraser looked at Stan to warn his colleague to stay out of the conversation. "This is hardly gossip, Beth. We're talking about the murder of two people. We need your cooperation."

"I want to cooperate, but I don't spread gossip," she said firmly.

The questioning continued for another hour with very little progress. Beth offered them more coffee, but they opted to go down the street to a shop where they could review their impressions in private.

Fraser spoke as they left. "Could we ask you to keep this conversation between the four of us? We'd rather you didn't share any of the questions with Ron."

Beth looked briefly at Stan and turned back to Fraser. "If that's what you want."

In the restaurant, Brad said, "Pretty quiet life here. Play golf. Go to Wellesley. Go to a bridge tournament. Sell some bonds when you need cash."

"Watch your back at all times," said Stan.

Fraser was all for digging a little deeper. "I wonder why Johnson was so agreeable about us using his office. Then he disappears for a couple of hours."

"Could he have a tape recorder going in there?" wondered Brad.

"You could have a look while we're talking," said Stan. "It would have to be somewhere out in the open; otherwise, it wouldn't pick up much."

"If Johnson gets back before we do, he'll have it well tucked away," said Fraser. "We could ask him outright. Or maybe ask Beth if he ever uses one. It's hard to get her to open up. Stan, you seem to have more luck prying information out of her than the rest of us."

Stan looked momentarily embarrassed.

Fraser continued. "She lets on that she's very concerned about not gossiping, and it reaches the point where she is hardly passing on information we desperately need. We could improve our chances a lot, maybe even shorten this case, if we got the locals to be more candid with us."

"Maybe we ought to scare her a bit," suggested Macvey. "Threaten her with arrest."

"That would be clever," snapped Stan. "Give her every reason to bring in a lawyer."

"We're not ready for threats," said Fraser. "It would be a giant step forward if we could find another way to cultivate her and get more out of her."

Macvey said, "If you ask me, he's more interested in getting something into her." Stan's vicious look did nothing to diminish Macvey's amusement.

At that moment, Beth popped her head into their booth in the restaurant. "Ron's back if you want to talk to him."

On the way back to the office, Fraser decided that seating Johnson in a commanding position in the office would be a flawed strategy compared to the previous interview. Having Beth in the chair was obviously a bit of a joke, but having Johnson there would reduce the pressure Fraser liked to impose on those he interviewed, especially suspects. As they entered the office, Macvey surprised him by surging forward and taking the seat behind the desk. Johnson's face showed that he was upset by this maneuver, but he said nothing.

"I always wanted one of these chairs," Macvey said. "I wish the New York state police would get us some for our offices."

Fraser could hardly contain a smile. "I need one more than you do," he said, rubbing his backside.

When they were all seated, Fraser began the same old questions. "Tell us what you can about the Laches," he said. "Don't worry about repeating yourself. Stan here will sort out the testimony when he edits his notes."

Johnson started out with a frown. "I guess you know we were headed for San Antonio. Harry and Louise were driving down, leaving on the Tuesday. I flew down on Thursday of that week and we were supposed to play in the charity team game on Thursday night. Lugner and I met at the hotel. We flew separately. Harry and Louise didn't show up and I called Beth to see if she knew anything, if there'd been any change of plans. She said she knew nothing. I got her to call the state police and they checked the house. The car was gone, of course, and there was no sign of the Laches. That's it. Ted and I came home. We can't play together — don't get along at all. Anyway, neither of us felt like playing with the Laches' disappearance hanging over us."

"So you came back to Erieville and it was business as usual?" asked Fraser.

"Not exactly," said Johnson. "You can hardly have business as usual when the head of the company leaves the scene. All of the official documents that needed his signature were left hanging. I had to get a lawyer involved and get matters set up so that I could officially execute the papers."

"Who was the lawyer?" asked Stan.

"Frank Gittel," said Johnson. "You wouldn't know him. He handled all of Harry's, that is, the company's work."

"We'll want to talk to him. I assume he's still around?"

"He is. Just down the street. I'll introduce you."

"Okay," Fraser said. "Let me sum up the picture you're giving us. You get back from San Antonio. You talk to your lawyer and between you smooth over any business difficulties. At some point, you are able to take over ownership of the business."

"You make it sound like I had everything planned. What really happened was that the Laches left me the business in their will. I had to have some kind of authority to keep the business afloat. It would have been crazy to let an asset like this go down the drain through negligence or just plain laziness. After a period of three years following their disappearance, they were declared legally dead. At that time, I took over ownership. This office, the furniture, everything came to my name."

"You say the Laches' will," said Fraser. "Isn't it more accurate to say Mrs. Lache's will?"

"Sorry. That's what I meant."

"You ran the business for three years without the owner. Then you took over everything. All of the assets?"

"Right."

"I assume you made some money, that is, the firm made some money over those three years."

"Sure we did."

"What happened to that money? Those earnings?"

"They came to me, of course. During that three year period, the earnings just went into an account the firm has for retained earnings. I invested the money in bonds, like I always did when Harry was alive."

"So that money came to you as well?"

"Of course it did. It was part of the assets of the firm. Why shouldn't it?"

"I'm not saying it shouldn't. I was just curious as to why it wouldn't be declared a dividend and paid to other shareholders or beneficiaries of the Lache estate."

"Look, everything I did was perfectly legal. Ask Gittel."

Fraser continued. "At the moment, our concern is solving two murders. Did you spend much time at the Lache place on Wellesley Island?"

"Sure. We had a few weekends each summer up there. We played a lot of rubber bridge."

"Who was included?"

"Harry and Louise. Ted was always there. A neighbor, Lucy Dinde, came for a while, but she got turned off by the game."

"Just the four of you? Exchanging money among your foursome?"

"No. A couple named Hill — Bob and Marilyn — were regulars, too. They're from Pennsylvania somewhere and have a place on the island. Whenever they were around, they'd stop in and play."

"Were they big losers?" asked Fraser.

"The Hills are good card players," replied Johnson. "They loved to play a social form of bridge and never objected to playing for money. Harry would set the stake as high as possible, especially when he thought he had a pigeon. Ten cents a point was reasonable and to everyone's surprise, the Hills didn't protest. Even more surprising was that neither of the Hills was a pigeon. They knew little and cared less about modern bidding conventions. To them, the purpose of playing the game was to sort out who were the best players. They never bid grand slams and, in fact, seldom bid slams of any kind, but they went to game on every hand they could sniff a chance. I think they were very small losers over the long haul."

"Practical players," commented Fraser.

"They were," said Johnson. "Bob is nobody's dummy. He made it very clear that table talk was not allowable. He never threatened to leave the game, never even raised his voice. He'd just tell Ted and Harry something like, 'Cut that out,' or 'If you've got a bad cold, Harry, take some medicine. I can't stand the sound of your voice when you do that.' Hill is a really good poker player too. He'd shame Ted and Harry into an understanding and while their main pastime was bridge, they'd devote an occasional evening to poker. To make it easy for everyone, Bob and Marilyn took us all out on their yacht. It's a beauty too. They took us on overnight cruises of the Thousand Islands. When the weather cooperates, there's no finer way to spend a day. The scenery is spectacular. They served great food and drinks, and the players more or less got along. Nobody turned down the offer of an evening poker game. I'm sure that Hill and his wife recovered any money they might have lost at the bridge table, and then some. Hill is a pretty good coffee-houser, and he knew exactly how to needle his opponents or create smokescreens. Habits that are taboo in bridge are fair game at poker. Harry and Ted realized they had no business complaining about the habits of a couple they had marked as pigeons.

"Besides, the Hills and Laches had a bunch of common interests. Bob is a keen golfer and Harry began including him in games whenever they were visiting Wellesley Island. Bob needed to invest his retirement savings and our firm was a natural choice."

"What about other players?" asked Fraser.

"There were a few others from the area that the Laches used to ask to join us. A judge, Peter Avery, was pretty regular. And John Parler from Ithaca came often. There were a couple of other good players who showed up occasionally. Maybe ten people all together that would show up over the summer."

"Who were the big winners?"

"I think I won more than anyone else. I knew all the players and all their quirks. Rubber bridge isn't a game of technical perfection. You figure out what your partner is doing, what the opponents are up to, and go for a plus when you can. You don't need the biggest plus on every hand to be a winner. And you have to be alert for penalties. That kills most weak players. Lache and Lugner won reg-ularly. They did pretty well together."

"They had a good partnership?"

"They played a lot together. They knew what the other was doing. Maybe a little too much. They psyched a lot. It never bothered me because I could almost always figure it out. Louise picked up on it most of the time, but it fooled most of the others. It backfired occasionally and cost them big when it did, but overall, they gained by it."

"Were Ted and Harry good friends?"

Johnson narrowed his eyes. "Funny you should ask that. They've known each other for over forty years. Their relationship seemed to cool off during the last few years. For a long time they were a genuinely affable pair — always chuckling and friendly to each other and everyone else. Something happened somewhere along the line and that all changed. They didn't seem to enjoy each other's company nearly as much."

"And how about Mrs. Lache? You played a lot with her over the years."

"I did. I liked her. She would never be considered one of the top players, but she held up her end."

"What was the financial arrangement between you and the Laches?"

"What do you mean by that? I worked for Lache for years."

"How about expenses at bridge tournaments?"

"Harry covered all the entry fees."

"And other travel? Hotel, meals?"

"I don't see how that's anyone's business."

"This is a murder investigation, Mr. Johnson," said Stan.

"Lugner was a client of the firm and Lache treated everything as business expenses. Tournaments were client entertainment."

"Is that legal?" asked Fraser.

"Not my problem," answered Johnson. "I wasn't about to tell my boss how to conduct his business. If the boss wants something, and the lawyer signs off on it, it's okay by me."

"Fine," said Fraser. "Back to Mrs. Lache. She was your regular partner and the four of you played in a lot of tournaments together. How many weekends a year would you say you played?"

"Oh hell, I don't know. Let's say we covered all the tournaments in Erieville, Syracuse, Buffalo, Rochester. We went to the occasional tournament in Ontario, Kingston, just across the lake. We went to a few national tournaments, not regularly."

"So what does all that add up to?"

"I guess twelve, fifteen weekends a year."

"And then you had the rubber bridge on Wellesley Island."

"Yes. That would be another two or three weeks a year."

"You must have known each other well, and gotten along quite well to spend all that time together. You never got tired of the arrangement?"

"I thought about leaving many times, believe me. But Harry paid me well. I love the bond business. It hasn't been so great the last four years, but we had many exceptional years. Harry made money. All his clients made a ton of money. I made some for myself. I love northern New York. You can't beat the summers here. Winters are something else, but I do some cross country skiing on weekends when I am not playing bridge. And Erieville is a great place to live."

"Of all the folks you mentioned who came up to Wellesley, is there anyone who held a grudge against the Laches?"

Johnson paused before answering. Fraser thought for a minute that he wasn't going to answer at all, but then Johnson began to mutter. "Let me see. Avery, never. Parler, no guts. Hill, never around. Lucy Dinde? Old man Gehl? They might, but this is just guesswork on my part."

"What about Lugner? You say he and Lache were cooling."

"They were, but they were such old friends. I can't see him harming them. And Ted was fond of Louise. He would never be violent with her. He was always a gentleman."

"How was your own relationship with the Laches? Did you always hit it off with both of them?"

"We had our disagreements over the years. Bound to. But we all got along fine, all things considered."

"Tell me about those things."

"You know bridge players. We all have arguments. Harry liked to lecture Louise and me. He didn't really know what he was talking about. Every close decision you encounter can go either way. If you consider alternatives, and I always do, you know damned well that your second choice could have been right. Harry got on our backs when things didn't go right. He was the boss, so I couldn't argue with him."

"That was a tough situation for you. I'm surprised you put up with it for so long. How about Mrs. Lache?"

"She wouldn't take anything from Harry. She defended my actions to him as well. She'd give him royal hell for the ridiculous results they came up with. Bad contracts, misplays, misdefenses."

"And how was your relationship? Did she ever question your actions?"

"At first, she accepted me as the teacher, but she began to focus on results rather than logic. She was getting harder and harder to play with as time went on."

"You must have been ready to abandon ship."

"Sure, I got totally fed up at times. But, what the hell, the pluses outweighed the minuses."

CHAPTER 7

Fraser arrived half an hour early at the school gymnasium where he was to meet Lugner for their game. Ted had promised to introduce him to some of the locals who had known the Laches. Fraser was disappointed when Lugner did not show up promptly. He saw Ron Johnson arrive a few minutes before game time and the two struck up a conversation.

"I didn't know you were going to honor us at our game tonight," said Johnson.

"Ted suggested it might be a good way to meet local people. I don't see him here, though. We were going to get together at six-thirty."

"Believe only part of what he tells you. He's getting a bit old and forgetful. That happens when you pass eighty."

Fraser's tempered flared and he began to have misgivings about the evening's venture. He wondered if he would have been better off spending the evening in his hotel room combing files trying to find an avenue worth exploring. When he remembered how barren the files really were, he realized that if he picked up any leads at all, any time spent at tonight's game would be worthwhile.

"You were regular teammates. You must know his game pretty well."

"I played on the same team, but never with him as partner. He and Harry were always partners and I played with Louise."

"How was his game?"

"He was solid. Still is, I imagine, although I haven't played at the same table for over a year. I'm surprised he wanted to come out."

"He suggested it," said Fraser. "I had other plans until I heard the idea."

"Here's someone you should meet," said Johnson. He introduced Art to Nori Wong, a petite, mature lady with a perfect complexion and fine features. Her black hair was tied back in a pony tail. The whole effect was striking and he found that he could hardly keep his eyes off her. She was obviously used to attention and smiled confidently at him. Johnson mentioned that Fraser was looking into the Lache deaths.

Nori spoke up immediately. "I saw in the paper that they found the bodies. What was it? Four years they've been there? Buried in bags and left to rot. The whole thing is disgusting. I hope you find whoever did it."

"That's what I'm here for," said Fraser. "You knew them well?"

"I played the odd game with Louise. I didn't know Harry all that well. He was way over my head. He'd never ask me for a game. But he was always so nice to me. Not like that old fool Lugner he played with regularly."

"Really," said Fraser.

"Careful, Nori," said Johnson. "He's Art's partner for tonight."

At that moment Lugner appeared in the doorway and the conversation terminated abruptly.

"Can I see you tomorrow morning?" Fraser asked Nori.

"We can meet after the game if you want."

Fraser noted her frown and slight sideways turn as she finished her invitation. "Maybe a few of us can go out after the game," he said.

"Okay," she replied curtly, and walked away.

Lugner ambled up and apologized for being late. "Sorry. I almost slept through the game." Lugner was wearing the same clothes as yesterday.

"No problem," said Fraser. "We'll have to use one of your old convention cards. I can play most anything you want."

"Good. Old fashioned is what I like."

As the evening progressed, Fraser developed a strange feeling about the atmosphere at the tables they visited. Lugner had suggested the game with the excuse that he could introduce Fraser to several of the players who knew the Laches. Yet Lugner was introducing him to very few of the opponents as they sat down, and only a few of the players greeted him by name. As they moved from table to table, it became evident that he was not a regular at the club. Even stranger, Lugner did not speak at all to several of the opponents, not even observing the common courtesy of muttering a greeting when they sat down at a new table. Fraser thought, *he has plenty of enemies in this crowd.*

In spite of the atmosphere, Fraser found himself enjoying the game. Lugner proved to be an excellent partner. Although his shuffling gait and his slumped posture gave the appearance of drowsiness, he seemed to miss very little in the bidding or play. They had one serious misunderstanding and Fraser apologized, but Lugner brushed it off.

"I didn't have to make that call," he said. "I half expected it would cause a problem. We were vulnerable, too, so it was pretty risky."

After the game, a group of a dozen players, including Nori, the club owner, and others, went to a wine bar two doors down from the club. Lugner declined to go along, pleading old age. Ron Johnson made himself invisible immediately after the game. The bar was evidently a favorite hangout for the players. The bartender quickly agreed on "the usual" for three or four of them and took orders from the others. They discussed a number of the hands played during the evening, focusing mainly on triumphs, hard luck stories and bidding questions. As bridge players habitually do, they had no hesitation involving a newcomer like Fraser in their conversation.

By the time they had finished the first round of drinks, everyone in the crowd had been introduced to Fraser and knew why he was in town. They began discussing the murder, quietly at first, and then, as Fraser had hoped, they engaged in rapid, off-the-cuff opinions on what had happened. Fraser sat next to Nori and focused on her conversation.

"Harry really had it on for Beth. They have a kid that she looks after. Doesn't live with her, but she visits regularly," she said.

Fraser covered his surprise by reaching for his glass.

"Really. How old is the child now?"

"She's a teenager now. Maybe fifteen or so. I'm not sure exactly. There's something wrong with the girl. Mental problems. The one time I met her was an accident. She couldn't have acting older than five."

Fraser relaxed. "Did you know Beth well?"

"Not really. She's lived here a long time and I've been here for twelve years. She doesn't play bridge at all, so our paths don't cross."

"How about Ron Johnson? You must see him at the bridge table a lot."

"We do see him now and then. Tonight's appearance was an exception. He's more of a tournament player than a club player. He thinks he's way above us and doesn't mix much. It puzzles me that he got hold of the Lache business. He doesn't come across as being that smart. I know he's a great bridge player, but he has no personality whatsoever. He couldn't sell a stock or a bond if his life depended on it."

"Interesting. Did Lache and Lugner play much at the club?"

"Old Ted and Harry stopped coming years ago. They reached a point where they fought every time they played. They couldn't play a hand without one of them insulting the other. I'm surprised they played in any tournaments after that."

Fraser sat in amazement, nursing his one light beer and making mental notes on the words he was hearing. Everything would need to be documented before he went to bed, lest they be forgotten, and followed up over the next couple of days. All of the partygoers were friendly and some offered to help. The club owner agreed to provide addresses for several of the players.

Nori lingered after the others and Fraser talked to her for a while longer. She told him that the city of Erieville had two main bridge clubs. At first, he thought this was evidence of growth in interest in bridge as a pastime, an event that went against the worldwide trend. Nori soon corrected his misguided guess. "No, nothing like that. We have two clubs in Erieville, but not because the game is getting more popular. We have two groups of players, and they're split right down the middle in every way. Players who go to Bill's club never go to Maggie's club. Bill and Maggie loathe each other. If they met casually on the street, one of them would likely end up in hospital."

"How did it start?" wondered Art.

"About ten years ago, just after I got to Erieville, they had a run-in over some insignificant matter. Maggie mentioned at a unit meeting that someone seemed to make a lot of money organizing sectional tournaments. Bill did all the organizing, has for years, and he took it as a personal insult. He flung it right back at Maggie and what started out as a friendly meeting turned into a verbal brawl."

"Bridge players can do that."

"They sure can. The players all took sides in the matter, and now we have two camps. With maybe a few exceptions, players in one camp won't go near the others. They play in tournaments without a fuss, but otherwise, they have nothing to do with each other."

"How strange. It would make a good case for a sociology course," said Fraser. "Do you just play here at Bill's club?"

"No. I'm one of the few who crosses the line. I play in both. I really like Bill and Maggie. I stay out of any discussions involving the two."

"What about Lugner? What's behind all the hostility between you two?" asked Art.

"Lugner knows exactly how I feel about him. He couldn't care less."

"What exactly has he done to you to make you feel that way?"

"Jason, that's my son, he works for him. He lives at Lugner's place. I hate the arrangement. There's nothing I can do about it."

"Your son lives at Lugner's place?" said Fraser.

"For almost five years now. I tried everything to talk him out of it, but the old bastard pays him so much to keep him around I don't get anywhere. There's nothing I can legally do either. Jason's old enough to make up his own mind."

Fraser sipped his beer. *That'd be the guy carrying wood into the garage. He's been close to Lugner for five years. I'll have to talk to him.* Then he smiled, his attention caught fully by the misery on Nori's beautiful face.

"I'm sorry that this is so upsetting to you. When did you last see the Laches?"

"I saw Louise the week before they were supposed to go to San Antonio. I hadn't seen Harry for at least a month before that."

"Remember anything unusual going on at the time?"

"No. Well, Ron remembers. They were going to play together in the team games in San Antonio. Louise was a little peeved at Harry."

When the conversation slowed, Fraser offered her a ride home.

"I have wheels," she said. "But if you want to have a game at Maggie's club some night, you could pick me up."

"That sounds fine. I'm only in town for a short spell, but if we can fit it in, I'd like that."

"Her game is every Tuesday."

"I'll pick you up then."

"Come by about five. We can have dinner at my place."

CHAPTER 8

On Friday morning the officers again met for breakfast in the Wellesley Island motel. Fraser said, "We've got a good day's work ahead. Brad has plans in Syracuse and I'm heading off to Buffalo around six."

Brad was talkative at first, eager to expand on his girlfriend and his hopes of continuing to impress her. "Sophie's a great lady. Nicest I ever met."

"What does she do?" asked Fraser.

"She works at the station in Syracuse. Really understands police work. She's so tuned in to my problems. That's one of the reasons I like her so much."

"You two are getting pretty serious. I might have to speak to Cameron and recommend that he transfer one of you out of the department if you get too involved."

"It'd be only fair then if I called your boss and explained your love life," responded Brad.

Fraser laughed. "Touché. We're better off talking about the neighbors on the island. We haven't found the key to unlock Lucy and Gehl. They give us bits and pieces, but it's like squeezing a dry lemon."

"That's how I feel," said Brad. There's not a lot for them to do all day except look after their places. Lucy has a decent-sized place and it keeps her pretty busy looking after it. The old guy, Gehl, his place isn't as big. It doesn't look like he does much to keep it in shape. Shabby. House and grounds both. You'd think they'd both be more interested in what goes on around them."

Fraser grunted in agreement.

"Someone shows up one night and buries a couple of bodies, you'd think they'd notice. It'd have to be done at night. Anytime during the day would be too obvious. It'd be hard work, with a lot of grunting and groaning. Seems hard to miss."

Macvey shrugged. "Four years is a long time to remember details, but I guess this wasn't just a detail. I wish we could think of something to jog their memories. Guess we have to keep hammering."

"Stan, you plan on staying around here, right?" Fraser asked.

Stan nodded, unwilling to divulge his half-formed plans.

"You may find something when you nose around on the weekend," continued Fraser. "We can catch up on Sunday night."

The drive to Buffalo was uneventful. Fraser cruised at seventy-five along Highway 81, and when he reached the New York turnpike, where the officers knew his car, he accelerated to his normal cruising speed, near ninety. A slight drizzle made the surface of the road a tiny bit slippery and anyone unfamiliar with Fraser's expert driving would have shuddered a few times watching his maneuvers. He stopped by his office building on the east side of Buffalo, checked his mail and called his bridge partner Stewart Appleton to make an appointment for lunch the following day.

Fraser also took the time to send an update to Bryder. It was a good opportunity for reflection, as he had to summarize his disjointed notes, which helped him to gain perspective. He laid out the main facts and noted the five suspects that were under investigation. The fact that he had no firm conclusions bothered him.

Bryder always came across as a cool individual. Although they had worked together for almost two years, no warmth had ever evolved in their relationship. Fraser respected Bryder as a professional, but he would never trust him with personal issues. Bryder was all business and his priorities lay in the direction of furthering his own career. As long as Fraser did his job well, he could be sure of Bryder's support. Otherwise, Bryder would follow the book, even at the expense of a colleague. Still, Bryder had never interfered with his investigations and Fraser assumed he would not do so on this occasion, so he offered details freely. He thought it would be a nice gesture to copy Alex Cameron on the note. The senior officers had a habit of checking email reports regularly and Fraser expected they would look over his report some time Saturday morning.

As he drove on to his apartment, towards Karen, his mind drifted away from the case and he pondered his own personal issues. He liked Karen a lot. She was always affectionate, often gently approaching him when his mind was elsewhere, lifting him out of his work problems and arousing him. She had become a diligent student of bridge to please him. Although not a star in a technical sense, she always seemed to know what was going on at the table. When she played frequently enough, this translated into real talent and had produced several excellent games for their partnership.

After his accident, she had shown compassion and skill in helping him get through the discomfort. His offer to go to Reno had generated a trace of excitement in her and after checking her work schedule she had accepted. All of these things had brought him closer to Karen than ever before. He now realized that Jill had sensed the real situation and decided it was time to terminate their triangle.

When he got to his apartment, Karen greeted him with a hug. She was wearing a tight black cashmere sweater and a short black skirt. The outfit suited her perfectly and felt softly appealing as he embraced her.

"Hungry?" she asked.

"Famished."

"A glass of wine?"

Art was not a big drinker and he hesitated at the offer.

Karen said, "We need to celebrate. This is the first evening we've had alone in our apartment in years."

He did not see Jill's departure as a cause for celebration, but the Karen's glow was contagious. He sensed that it would be terribly wrong to dissolve her happiness. The glow continued through the evening, accompanied by wine, dinner, their favorite music and then delicious intimacy.

Art's curiosity about the details of Jill's new home faded as the evening wore on. By the time he felt himself dozing off, he had pretty much decided he would postpone queries to a later date, perhaps much later.

— ♦ —

On Friday evening Stan went to an Erieville restaurant. Over a double bourbon and a steak, he reflected that his need for female companionship was becoming overpowering. A rendezvous with Beth would fill this need admirably. Saturday was a free day for him and he hoped for a little luck. Beth might have either an open schedule or one that could be opened with the right approach. She could hardly refuse a request to provide further information on a murder case. He could propose a meeting, probe for an excuse to spend a few hours with her, and apply some pressure if need be. If it turned out that she was truly busy, he had lost nothing. At the very least, he might be able to lay the foundation for a future liaison. He decided he would ask for an early appointment. If she had no fully formed plans for the day, or had some flexibility, he might be able to help her do the planning. He liked this idea so much that he skipped dessert, paid his bill and headed for a phone.

Beth was happy to meet him at ten the following morning. She had a few errands to run before that time and was thinking of playing tennis in the afternoon, but had no firm plans. That suited Stan perfectly.

In his motel that night, he gave the television a small part of his attention while he imagined the conversation he would have with Beth in the morning.

Early Saturday morning, he bounced out of bed, thinking that this was the old Stan, pursuing a possible conquest, and perhaps advancing the cause of the New York State Police at the same time. He wanted his appearance to be perfect — as perfect as a thin, sixty-eight-year-old man with thin lips, thin arms and thinning hair could manage. He shaved carefully, showered, scrubbed his teeth, gargled with mouthwash, selected an old but classic Harris Tweed jacket, and left out the tie. His flannels proved to need only a last minute press and his shoes a touchup shine to get them gleaming. He chuckled inwardly as he slipped not one but two small blue pills into a small ziplock bag and thence into an inner pocket of the tweed jacket. He vacuumed out his primitive BMW, front and back seats, cleaned the leather and restored a gleam to the mahogany panels. As he made his way to Beth's apartment, he congratulated himself with the thought that old Stan was leaving nothing to chance.

He sighted several recently arrived robins, a few nervous chipmunks beginning to venture out of their winter burrows, and a group of energetic squirrels playing tag. Tumescent bulbs and perennial shoots parted the crust of the earth, pressing upwards in anticipation of spring. His spirits soared.

— —

In the meantime, Brad was advancing his love life in his own way. The overtures from Lucy had stirred him mightily, but he knew he could never explain an absence to Sophie if he did not show for her birthday Friday evening. His problems were the reverse of Stan's. With Sophie, there was never a question of what the two would do over the weekend. The only question was how often. Brad was no teenage Romeo, and Sophie no Juliet, but the pair were genuinely fond of each other and had an unerring instinct for what they would do when they were alone. Sophie had a happy birthday indeed.

CHAPTER 9

The following morning Art Fraser rose early and cooked breakfast. Fried eggs, runny, two for him and three for Karen; Canadian bacon, two strips for him, and four for Karen, along with strong coffee and whole wheat toast. When the cooking neared completion, he could hardly wait to dig in.

"Lots to do today?" asked Karen.

"I'm going to meet Jack and Helen Duffy about nine. They knew the dead couple and might be able to give me some background. Then I'm going to see Stewart."

"I'm going shopping. We need replacements for some of the stuff I agreed to give Jill."

"Give Jill?"

"She has a right to her share. Not a lot. She contributed."

"Okay. I was thinking of personal things — pictures and the few bits of furniture."

"I said we'd split everything equally — three shares, one each. She's not trying to rip us off. She's picking up the kitchen set next week."

"The whole thing? Chairs and table? I bought that myself."

"And the dishes and silverware. I don't like them anyway. Time to clean them all out. She's taking all her bedroom furniture as well."

"That's the best deal we can make?"

"This wasn't a big haggling exercise, Art. I was trying to be fair. You weren't here, remember? I offered her these things. I know she likes them. She's paying for the mover."

"Thank goodness."

"Think of it this way. We get to keep the living room furniture, stereo, and all the CDs and tapes. I really like that furniture. Besides, I want us all to go on being friends. We had a pretty good time together right from police school 'til now. I wasn't going to nickel and dime her and break up our friendship."

"If you say so."

Stan Piper arrived at Beth's apartment block at two minutes to ten. She appeared in her tennis outfit: a short white skirt and a crisp white sleeveless blouse. Stan took a deep breath when he saw her and shook hands very carefully. She greeted him warmly, saying, "There's something I want to show you, if you can spare a moment."

"Of course." There were lots of things Stan wanted to see.

"My dishwasher is leaking and repair men are so expensive. Could you have a look?"

Under normal circumstances, Stan's interest in dishwashers would have been less than zero, and he would have declined such an invitation quickly and firmly. These were not normal circumstances, however. He agreed to be led into the kitchen.

"Careful," Beth said. "There's water on the floor. Make sure you don't slip."

She showed him the appliance, opened the door for his inspection, and Stan saw nothing that was obviously wrong with it.

"I'll need to get down there on the floor and have a look at the drains to see if I can find the problem. I'll need a towel and probably a screwdriver and a pair of pliers. Get a flashlight as well, if you have one."

"No problem." Beth produced the required items after some searching.

Stan laid the towel on the floor and spread himself out in a position where he could get at the water supply and drainage piping. He looked up to ask Beth to shine the flashlight on the pipes and flushed at the view. Her skirt revealed a startling amount of creamy skin. Stan looked quickly away, breathing heavily.

Beth cooperated willingly in getting light on the subject and he spotted a loose connection in the drainage tube. He asked Beth for the screwdriver, and in the process of reaching and delivering the item, she slipped on the wet floor and fell on top of him. Stan's elbow and back banged sharply against the ceramic floor, but a delicious feeling of contact with a warm body overwhelmed any desire to protest.

"Oh dear," said Beth. "I didn't mean to do that. Are you all right?"

"No problem," said Stan valiantly, doing everything possible to prolong the moment and to avail himself as much as possible of any opportunities to feel the best way out of the situation.

When Beth put both hands on the floor to get the leverage she needed to rise, Stan could no longer help himself. He kissed her.

"Oh my," said Beth, pulling reluctantly away.

"Sorry," said Stan, not feeling sorry at all.

He kissed her again. She kissed him back. Stan wished now that he taken one of his little blue pills earlier. With more self-control than he believed possible, he disentangled them and helped Beth to her feet. He squeezed her hand and prepared for their interview.

Fraser was correct in his assumption that the mail he sent out on Friday would be looked at on Saturday morning. Alex Cameron, in charge of a much smaller unit than Gordon Bryder, had plenty of time to become engrossed in the details of cases that were active under his authority. He carefully examined the details in Fraser's note and in turn sent it along to his superior, George Marshall, in Albany. Marshall was second in command of the regional New York State group and had responsibility for upstate counties. After reading Fraser's note, Marshall called Cameron.

"You're making progress on the Lache case."

"We've gone from nowhere to a small step forward. There are so many missing parts I'm not holding my breath."

"A four-year-old case with no real evidence is a tough assignment."

"That's what Fraser keeps telling me."

"I wonder if you shouldn't be putting heat on that guy Ron Johnson. I can't help thinking that he might be your man. He had the most to gain by the murder. He got the whole brokerage business when the Laches died. Nobody else had that kind of motive. Follow the motive, I've always figured."

"I'm sure Fraser has taken that into account. None of the suspects is the type to disappear. If Johnson's the man, Fraser will get to him." Cameron was trying to figure a way to intervene in the case and at the same time to shower a little credit on himself should this thread lead to a resolution. "Leave this with me, sir. There may be something there. I'll mull it over and maybe give it a little push."

Cameron called Gordon Bryder as soon as he finished his conversation with

Marshall. Bryder took the opportunity to question Cameron on the quality of help Fraser was getting. "I give you my best man and you assign a rookie and a has-been to help out."

Cameron knew that his old friend was not overly troubled by the situation. "Excellent training for Fraser," he replied. "A good man can handle it. Macvey knows the islanders. They're unique. He fits right in. He'll get more cooperation that any five of my other officers. Anyway, I don't have five detectives to assign. Stan Piper is far from a has-been. He's not a young man, but he's not afraid of work. This isn't Buffalo where you've got manpower coming out your ying yang."

"We all get what we deserve."

Alex finally got an opportunity to raise the subject he had in mind. "I looked over Fraser's email. Good of him to keep us in the picture."

"Standard practice in Buffalo," replied Bryder.

"I can't help thinking he dug up some important facts relating to the motive."

"What about revenge?"

"I'm thinking financial gain at the moment. Look at Johnson. He got the whole damned brokerage business when the Laches departed. He had more to gain than anyone. I think we need to put a little heat on him. What do you say?"

"Alex, I wouldn't butt into Fraser's investigation. If you want to make a little suggestion, no problem. If you want to start ordering the man around, you're cutting into his effectiveness. I wouldn't touch that."

"I'm not talking about ordering anyone around. I think we ought to talk up the idea that someone should question this man Johnson pretty carefully. He would be number one in my book. How could that hurt anything?"

"That's up to you. I'd wait until Fraser asks for help. He's not dumb."

"Well, I'm going to raise the subject with him." After he had hung up, Cameron wondered if it wouldn't look better if he merely bided his time and said nothing to Fraser. Then he thought, *I can work through Piper. That'll be easy. He'll listen to me. We'll turn this whole thing in the right direction.*

— —

Fraser looked forward to his meeting with Stewart Appleton. They had become good friends over the years and enjoyed chatting about many subjects. Heading the list was a good bridge hand or two, followed by a discussion of the personalities and bridge abilities of the people involved. Today, he was after specifics — the Laches. Stewart was well known at a small restaurant near his club and the good service he and friends always received was a bonus.

"You took off to Erieville pretty quickly after we got back from Reno," said Appleton. "So they found Lache."

"And his wife. They figure they've been dead four years — murdered about the time they disappeared. Buried on the property where they had a summer home. How well did you know them?"

"I knew them for years. I liked Louise a lot. Harry, well, he was a blusterer. Pretty good player. For a long time, years ago, Lache played with a guy called Lugner —"

"That'd be Ted. I've already met him."

"Okay. You know him. He and Harry were regular partners. You remember Hermann? The guy who was killed a couple of years back? Great card player, old-fashioned bidder."

"How could I forget him?"

"I played a lot with Hermann at one time and eventually we got hooked up with Lache and Lugner. For a while they wanted us to play with them regularly, but Hermann resisted. If he took a dislike to someone, he wanted nothing to do with them. We played with them once. Only once. After that, Hermann absolutely refused to play in anything with them. They eventually quit asking us."

"What was Hermann's problem?"

"He claimed they were cheating. He didn't come right out and say it. He just gestured, imitated them. It was a hoot to watch his little circus. He could imitate their facial expressions, their bids, doubles, tone of voice, where they put the emphasis. He was tuned in to everything they did, stuff that casual players never notice, but Hermann picked up on it right away. As soon as he mentioned it, I started to watch for it and I could see it too. Plainly cheating. Nothing you could go to a committee about. Very subtle stuff. But once you were onto it, you noticed it every time."

"Small-time cheaters. I often wonder why people cheat at bridge."

"Maybe you know what W.C. Fields said: 'If it's worth having, it's worth cheating for.' Cheating is a pretty widespread element of human behavior."

Fraser grunted.

Stewart continued. "For quite a while Lache and Lugner were the terror of northern New York tournaments. They won regularly in whatever they played — pairs games, team games. They were almost unbeatable in board-a-match games. Nobody would ever accuse them of being good bidders. Two-way Stayman, regular Blackwood and lots of penalty doubles, that was their repertoire. Before bidding boxes came out in the early eighties, they had a lot of tone of voice nuances going for them.

"None of the players they came up against faulted them for their habits. I don't think anybody noticed them. In a duplicate pairs game, you play only two or three hands against one pair and then move on to the next, and you don't get much opportunity to study the mannerisms of your opponents. Lache and Lugner were personable and popular. They were approachable, full of simple humor and laughed at everyone's jokes. They seemed to be enjoying themselves all the time. The mannerisms, hesitations and so on, they just seemed natural. A minute hesitation in pulling a pass or a double card would hardly be noticeable to a casual observer, but in a really experienced partnership it can be a big deal. It can signal the difference between a "standup double" and a close, doubtful bid. A confident slap of the cards can show good values for a bid.

"A cheat who misbehaved and insulted opponents would have drawn attention to his habits and begged scrutiny of his mannerisms. Not so with these guys. They were among the best-liked pairs in their bridge circles."

"Except in Hermann's opinion," remarked Fraser.

"That's right," agreed Appleton. "To Hermann, it was all transparent. After fifteen years of running a club, I've learned to pick most of that stuff up. I see it in club players all the time. Most players have mannerisms. They don't always do these things intentionally. A good poker player makes a living by picking up on tiny quirks. They work hard to get a read on everyone at the table. Hermann was that way. He saw through everything."

"Anything else you can tell me?"

"Now that you mention it, there is something. Rumors fly around. There was a story circulating years ago and I am sure it's mostly true. I heard that Harry and Ted were banned from a club a few years back. A rubber bridge club in New York City. That would be sometime in the late seventies when it was still operating.

They made a trip to New York City to try their hand at a high stake game. Many of the players there were tournament regulars and knew them. Lache and Lugner had no difficulty making the necessary arrangements to get into a game. Their ability compared to the run-of-the-mill players who showed up would have been below the average, that is to say they should have been regular losers. What saved them was the fact that they played together one rubber in three, and in that third rubber, their partnership agreements and mannerisms helped them out and they held their own.

"A lot of the great players used to show up there. The regulars were some of the most talented in the world. You could go in and kibitz Fishbein and Schenken, maybe B.J. Becker, all in the same game. They had few peers when it came to sensing what was going on at the table. If someone was cheating, they caught on within a few hands. Lache and Lugner were told bluntly that they weren't welcome to come back."

"Quite a story."

"While we're on gossip, there was some buzz about Lugner and Lache having a falling out a few years back."

"I thought they were the best of friends."

"That's what everyone says, and it's true for the most part, but most friends have arguments, sooner or later. Did you know that Lugner is gay?"

Fraser blinked. "No, I didn't know. I might have suspected. There's no sign of a female presence around his old house in Erieville." Fraser thought, *that explains why Nori is so upset about her son.*

"Anyway, the tournament regulars who show up at my club told me about some pretty good arguments Harry and Ted got into. They'd always gotten along pretty well for years. I was a little surprised to hear they were quarreling."

"What about? Bridge arguments?"

"Yes, bridge arguments, but not so much pointing out blunders. I'm talking about the kind of argument you get when one player, or both, loses respect for the other. I understand that Harry found out that Ted was gay some years after they had become friends. Years ago, gay people kept their habits in the closet. They told no one."

"That was the norm, for sure," said Fraser.

"I guess Harry was a homophobe or something close. He kidded Ted mercilessly. Poor Ted just sat there and took it for a while. Then he started on Harry's case. Harry ran after women. I'm not sure how many he went after. Probably nobody except Harry could tell you. Ted got his innings in. At some point they started criticizing each other's bridge judgment. Close judgments are part of the game. Sometimes we're right and other times a bid or play is dead wrong. But you can't fault partner for giving it his best shot and being wrong. That's the kind of situation they got into. They were questioning each other's judgment all the time."

"Pretty ugly, for a pair of old friends."

"Yeah. They got to know each others' personal lives too well after all those years of playing together and living in the same small town."

"What about this guy Johnson?"

Stewart shrugged dismissively.

"I don't know him well. A straight arrow, as far as I know. Terrific player. Very, very good. Technically, the best of that bunch."

Jack and Helen Duffy lived in a suburb of Buffalo and were regulars on the bridge circuit in New York State. Jack was an accountant who ran his own firm, well to do, and able to take time to play in as many bridge tournaments as he wanted, except during the tax season. Jack had been a prime suspect in the murder of Bob Smithers a few years earlier. His low boiling point had made it difficult for Fraser and his fellow officers to clear him quickly, but obviously he should never have been a suspect. Helen was a beautiful, gracious woman, whom Fraser especially admired. The couple had become good friends of Art's after the Smithers case. Art knew that women often had more insight into personal matters than men and expected that Helen would be particularly helpful in shedding light on the Laches' background.

They greeted him warmly at the front door and invited him inside. Helen gave him a hug before disappearing into the kitchen. When she returned with a tray of small sandwiches, they spent a pleasant half hour catching up on each other's lives. Naturally the conversation shifted to Art's work on the Lache case.

"So the reason for the Laches disappearance has finally been uncovered," said

Helen. "We used to see them all the time in New York state tournaments. Then whoosh, all of a sudden they were off the map."

"Their remains were found buried in what used to be their property on Wellesley Island. They've been there pretty close to four years. I'd be interested in any recollections either of you have about them."

"They were popular," said Jack, sharing a look with his wife.

"I liked Louise. Not Harry," Helen said. "He was a phony, as far as I could see. He was always laughing and friendly, but there was something under the surface that I never liked."

"Too rich," suggested Jack.

"Louise was losing her respect for him, too. She had an affair going with the guy who played on their team, Johnson. He's from Erieville too. The four of them always played together — the Laches, Ted Lugner and Ron Johnson. Lugner is still around. So is Johnson. But the team broke up. Disappeared is more like it, I guess."

"They were a tough team, too," said Jack. "Very hard to beat. They won a lot of tournaments around here."

"Tell me more about Johnson," said Art.

"Gossip, is that what you said?" asked Helen, with her eyes twinkling.

Art smiled back and nodded. "Exactly. Everything."

"He and Louise definitely had a thing going for quite a while. Harry ran around quite a bit. He even propositioned me one day."

"Anything in a skirt," said Jack, snorting.

"I like to think he was after quality," retorted Helen, laughing. "But yes. He went after a lot of women. He didn't try to hide it much either. We all knew about it. As for Louise, I don't blame her a bit for finding someone who liked her."

Jack stood up and began pacing the room. "Relationships in the world of bridge are probably no different than in any other social group. The big difference with bridge players is that there's less pressure to conform to any specific code of behavior. I think it's because people at the bridge table act in a less inhibited way than they do in other parts of their lives. We don't have any Emily Posts to listen to. There aren't any unnatural rules to follow, like you have in a church or a business, or even a golf club. Relationships form and break up easily. You see some partnerships that last for years, but they're the exception."

Helen added, "The manners of people in competitive bridge are pretty unique. If you feel like you're angry, you act angry. If you want to wear jeans and a great T-shirt, along with a black hat, that's what you do. You play against people for twenty years and the first time you meet them, they might say hello. For the next nineteen years, they're invisible. You meet them in the hall and they walk right by without acknowledging your existence. You play against them and they don't look at you. Say nothing. Of course, there are a few pros who are outgoing, always joking around, but they aren't the norm. Lache's team was like that for the most part — they were fun to play with."

Jack said, "Some rules about zero tolerance of bad behavior were introduced a few years ago. They're hard to enforce, and most people don't bother to complain. Ted and Harry could get ugly to one another, but not to their opponents. I doubt that anyone complained about them."

Art stretched and gratefully took another small sandwich from the platter Helen held out to him.

"So it sounds like this team of Louise, Harry, Ted and Ron had a great run for many years and then the wheels came off," said Art. "The relationships got all tangled up. Friends became enemies, colleagues cheated on one another. Their behavior towards one another changed completely over time."

"You might look at it that way," said Helen. "In this case, you had people with tons of money who had every option open to them. They chose different ways to deal with their problems. Maybe even going so far as to stoop to murder."

Fraser nodded.

"Johnson readily admits that he made out very well in the will the Laches left. He got the firm, including the building, the furniture and the accumulated profits."

Jack returned to the couch and sat down beside Helen.

"I hadn't heard. That would make him a multi-millionaire right now."

"He doesn't dress like one, but I guess he qualifies otherwise," said Art.

"He dresses like a bridge player," said Helen. "He wears whatever he feels like."

"Johnson benefited from a good-sized financial windfall. On the surface, that looks like a strong motive, but he's such a meek guy that I can hardly imagine him as a killer. And none of the neighbors has a strong motive for the murders. All we know is that somebody had a grudge against one or both of the Laches and that it was powerful enough to motivate a killer to dispense with both of them."

"There could be some sort of revenge motive that you don't know about," suggested Jack.

"Could be. We'll have to keep digging, because so far we have nothing concrete to go on."

After exchanging a few more pleasantries, Art indicated that it was time for him to leave. Jack stood up and accompanied him to the door.

"After all these years, it must be really tough to put together a picture of what happened."

Art grimaced, agreed, and let himself out.

CHAPTER 10

Fraser got a call from Brad Macvey about 8 a.m. on Sunday morning. "Hey Art, you're gonna have to get up here real quick," he said.

"What's up?" asked Fraser.

"We've got two more bodies for you. The Hills got in from Allentown Friday, as near as we can figure. Their bodies were found in their place early this morning. Both of them. Their skulls were caved in. Somebody smashed them up pretty good. Hit them several times."

"Where are you now?" asked Fraser.

"I'm up on Wellesley Island, at the Hill's place. Gehl got hold of me. He was out and about early this morning and he noticed something fishy next door. He went over to look. The front door was wide open, which he couldn't figure at all, so he just looked in and there they were."

"Damn. We'll have to shut the place down. The whole yard and the house. Does anyone else know?"

"Yeah. I phoned Stan and he says to let us know what you want to do. He was going to call Cameron. I already got the place marked off with yellow tape. I'll hang around until you get there."

"Okay, Brad. Good job. Can you get hold of the coroner and get him up there to do his thing?"

"I figured you'd want that. I'll call him soon as we hang up."

"I'll be there about two o'clock, maybe a little later," said Fraser.

"I thought you said you were a fast driver," said Brad.

"I have a couple of errands to do first," replied Fraser. "And I have to let Gord Bryder know what's happening."

"Cameron may have done that already. Anyway, I'll see you when I see you."

— —

About mid-morning, Stan was pleased to hear Alex Cameron's voice when he answered his cell phone.

"Hi, Stan. You have some news for me?"

"We've got a couple of more bodies to deal with."

"Two?" queried Cameron.

"Yes, Brad came across the Hills earlier this morning. He says the site's pretty clean, except for the bodies. They were lying in their house, both skulls smashed in. Nobody around and no obvious evidence. Fraser's in Buffalo. Brad's contacting him now. I'm heading for the site now."

Cameron said, "That certainly changes the whole picture up there."

"Absolutely. We were just slogging along on an old case. Now we've got a whole new ballgame."

"How do you see the situation?"

"It feels like we've been going in circles. We've got five suspects for the original pair of murders. We looked into the niece at the time of the disappearances and she came out clean. She isn't in town now, so she can't have been involved with the Hills murders. So we're left with the same group we're investigated already. Two are neighbors and they seem pretty harmless. A third is a woman, and I can't see her doing it. The other two guys, I don't know. One is so old he'd have a hell of a time swinging pipes and dragging bodies around. The other guy, Johnson, he could be the one. He seems like a wimp, though. Quiet as hell. I can't see him screwing up enough courage to kill someone. I wouldn't say we're anywhere near arresting anyone."

"You doing okay yourself?"

"Up till now, I've been doing what you pay me for, and I appreciate the work. Fraser is decent to operate with."

"Have you put some thought into the motive behind the killings? Didn't Johnson get the whole Lache brokerage business?" asked Cameron, knowing exactly what the answer was.

"He sure did. He's the only one with a cut-and-dried motive to kill them."

"If I was in your boots, I'd put a lot of time into Johnson — his alibi, his opportunity to do the job."

"We're going over everything pretty carefully. I'll make sure we don't miss anything related to Johnson's affairs."

"You don't need to mention this to Fraser. I'm just keeping myself tuned in," said Cameron. "Follow the motive. That has always been my guideline. Still is."

Fraser did his morning tasks, called Bryder, packed and hustled off for Wellesley Island. The murder of the Hills puzzled him. He had been counting on getting some testimony from them that would help with the Lache case. Obviously, he had been on the right track there. It looked as though the Hills knew something that the murderer did not want disclosed. What on earth could that be? One thing was certain. The cold case had just been transformed into a hot one. And he was the man in the hot seat. Surely Cameron and Bryder could not refuse to give him some real help now.

He stopped at a service station just before the Thousand Islands bridge to gas up his thirsty vehicle and put in a call to Cameron.

"We're lucky to have you on the case," said Cameron. Fraser thought, *and I'm damned unlucky. Nobody around that I know and trust. I have no clout with any of the locals, and now there's no time limit on my assignment.*

"We'll need some help to get this all sorted out," said Fraser. "I expect you'll assign a couple of full-time detectives to the team."

"I've already approved Stan as a full time member of your squad for as long as you need him. And Macvey is with you permanently until you wrap it up."

"I mean a couple of criminal investigation detectives with homicide experience."

"You won't find better people than Piper and Macvey. The other three detectives in this county are already assigned to cases. I'll do the best I can to help you. We need you to get to the bottom of this, and quickly. You must understand that we don't have unlimited funds and I don't have manpower sitting around unoccupied. My hands are tied."

He's a damned politician, thought Fraser. *What could I expect? I had no leverage with anybody coming in here, and I have none now.*

He hung up, paid for his gas and drove his Firebird to the Hill property. Yellow tape blocked the laneway and he had to park along the road in front of the yard. Macvey came over to report. "Doc Atlee says he'll be here about four o'clock. That's the best he can do. He's sending a local guy over for two o'clock. You're early."

"Damn," said Fraser. "I like Atlee. Is Stan coming up?"

"You said you'd be here at two. He'll be here then, I expect."

"I bloody well hope so. We've got a lot of work to do. Did you find anything of interest on the site?"

"I wouldn't say that. The bodies are inside the door. Nothing's been moved. Gehl says he didn't do anything, just looked in, saw the bodies, and called me. He's still at his place, expecting us to drop over."

Fraser asked if any clues had shown up in the yard.

Macvey said, "I've already had a pretty good look while I was waiting. There are tire tracks in the grass beside the laneway. Not good enough for a plaster cast, but maybe Stan can get some photos that we can do something with. He has a digital camera. I expect he'll be more than happy to take a bunch of photos."

Stan drove up at this point and came over to where Fraser and Macvey were talking. He was followed within minutes by a young man who introduced himself as a Doctor Delfan, appointed by the coroner. "Glad to have you," said Fraser. "Let's take a look at what we've got."

Delfan proved to be a capable, thorough practitioner, in spite of his evident youth. He took charge of the crime scene and ordered the three officers around as though he were a drill sergeant. There were two bodies close together on the kitchen floor. They had obviously been repeatedly bludgeoned by a similar blunt implement. There was little visible blood and nothing in the room out of its normal order. Delfan took several photographs and intoned statements regularly into a tape recorder as they inspected the bodies. When he had finished, Delfan said, "Can you help me load the bodies into my van? I'm going to take them to one of the funeral homes we use for a morgue in Erieville. Doc Atlee is meeting me there and we'll go over my notes. I understand he's coming here later."

As they watched Delfan's van drive off, Stan waved a camera case. "I thought this would be of some use to us," he said. "I can get plenty of pictures for us. Of course, the doc got quite a few, but we may find things of interest besides the bodies."

"Fine," said Fraser.

When he spotted the differences in the tracks on the grounds of the Hill property, Stan thought he saw a ripe field. Fraser inspected the spot Stan was indicating and although he could hardly see it at first, when he looked from a different angle, the light disclosed a pretty clear section of tire track in the grass. They moved over a couple of feet and found another, even less clear, but unmistakable track.

Stan had filed away a magazine article that explained the different tread designs of several current tire models. Grooves, ribs, symmetry, width; these were all aspects of the tire that he understood. Now, if he could just take some digital pictures of the imprints the tires had made on the soft soil, he could compare the details to the pictures in his magazine and work out what kind of tires were involved. That might lead to identification of a vehicle, which in turn might be a giant step forward in solving the case. He moved about with his camera like a man with an important mission, snapping pictures from several different angles. A few minutes later he called Fraser over.

"This is just like reading a golf green," said Stan. "Look at it with the light behind you and you can see it clearly. The photo is clearer from this side, too. You can see the difference between these and the Hills' Buick. We just need to track down the type of tire and that'll tell us the make of car."

Fraser had spent several years tracking stolen vehicles before he took an assignment in homicide. From this background he knew that the marks would lead them to the type of tire, but they would have to be very lucky to trace them to a particular vehicle and thence to an owner. He thought, *from the way he's going at it, you'd think he's going to solve the case right now.* He said, "A lot of cars use the same tires. Replacement brands go on any type of vehicle." Stan didn't reply and Fraser left him to his probably futile work.

— —

Stan, true to his reputation of being a bulldog, took measurements of the tire track traces in the grass, faint as it was, and recorded them in his notebook. He thought he might need a sample of the wet earth in the yard near the spot where he had found the tire tracks, and collected a handful in a plastic bag. *Maybe a lab can make something of this,* he thought. Then he took his memory chip to a one-hour photo dealer in Erieville and had prints made. He was pleased to see how clear some of the photos looked. With these in hand he visited a tire dealer in Erieville.

"The tread and width of that item definitely looks like a Goodyear Eagle," said the service man. "They're an original equipment model, used mostly on Chrysler products. Three Hundred, Concorde, Intrepid. That tire would be a little big for other Chrysler cars, but they might be used on trucks as well. They could be used on other makes, too, but I'm sure of the ones I quoted. The others are guesswork."

"I'll start with Chrysler then," said Stan, gratified. "Thanks for your help. I may need to call you later."

His next stop was the Chrysler dealer in Erieville. He knew one of the salesmen there and had remained on friendly terms with him. "What do you know about tires, Rudy?" he asked.

"Everything I need to know," replied Rudy Oltar. "What do you need to know?"

"What vehicles use Goodyear Eagles?"

Oltar repeated the tire serviceman's report.

"No trucks?" asked Stan.

"Not original equipment. Replacements maybe."

"Okay. Can you tell me of any local, I mean Erieville residents, who bought a Three Hundred, a Concorde, or an Intrepid over the past four years?"

"Whoa right there. I'm supposed to sell cars, not provide data to inquisitive passersby."

"I'm working on a murder, Rudy. Want me to check with your boss?"

"No need to do that."

"How about I drop by tomorrow morning?"

"Fine."

CHAPTER 11

First on Fraser's agenda on Monday morning was a visit to Lache's office for a talk with Beth and Johnson. He could call Lugner from there to make sure he would be available right after lunch. When he arrived at the office shortly after ten, Beth was at work on a stack of papers in the office.

"I need to ask you a few more questions," said Fraser, now speaking in a crisp, business-like tone that reflected his impatience with the circular way the witnesses were answering his questions. "Is Johnson in?"

Beth picked up the difference in tone and sounded resentful as she said, "I wish you had phoned first. Ron will be in later. All my quarterly statements are due," she said, pointing to the pile of paper. "Could you drop by tomorrow?"

"Sorry," replied Fraser. "This can't wait. I won't need more than an hour."

Beth looked around helplessly and saw that she had no choice. "You can handle the complaints I get for late reports. Let's go into the conference room."

When they had seated themselves on opposite sides of the table, Fraser noted that their voices sounded strange in the large room, and he got a feeling of a huge distance between them. Beth did not offer any coffee this time around. "I understand that you and Lache had a more intimate relationship than you wanted to talk about at first," he said.

Beth blushed deeply. "Who told you?"

"I need you to tell me everything," said Fraser. "I don't want to come back seven or eight times, and you don't want us bothering you for the next month."

"Don't I have any rights?" she asked, now on the verge of sobbing. "Maybe I should get a lawyer."

Fraser continued to press her. "You have every right to get a lawyer. At the moment, you are not accused of anything and you might waste a lot of your own money. I'm looking for facts, that's all. I'd like you to be a little more open than the first time we talked."

"The first time we talked I wasn't alone," she reminded them. "Do you expect someone to talk about personal matters in a crowd? I suppose you'd like to start a pretty good gossip line."

"Everyone in the group was a police officer and part of the same team investigating what has now grown to four murders. Nothing you tell me will go any further unless it relates directly to the murders we're investigating. Now, please, let's get on. Tell me about your relationship with Lache."

"All right. I met him several years ago. I finished college and was looking for a job. I wanted to live some place in upper New York. Harry needed someone to look after his books, be a receptionist, do odd jobs, whatever. It was just what I wanted. I never wanted to work for a big company. He and Louise treated me well. I got to like Harry, and well, we had an affair."

"You had a child?"

Beth blushed again. "Yes," she sighed. "Jeanie. He gave me money for her. That all stopped when he disappeared."

"He made no provision in his will?" asked Fraser.

"None. Louise found out about it eventually. Naturally, she was furious. We'd been pretty good friends until then. I can't blame her. I felt really guilty about the whole situation."

"You still went up to Wellesley Island with him?" asked Fraser.

Beth looked away. "Yes I did," she said, whispering now. "Harry always wanted me to go with him. He was so persuasive, and he was fun to be with."

Fraser felt he was nearing the end of useful questions with Beth when he heard the front door to the office open. They heard Johnson shout, "Hi Beth. Got visitors?"

Fraser came out of the conference room wearing the same grim look he had put on earlier and said, "Hello. You're just in time. Come on in."

Beth returned to her stack of papers and Johnson entered the meeting room. "Good morning. How can I help?"

Fraser said, "We're going over the gaps in our information. I'd like to flesh out the details of the testimony we have so far."

"I thought we gave you everything," said Johnson.

"Not quite. In fact, there are several gaps in the story you passed on to us. Let's start with your relationship with Louise. Tell us all about it. Everything, this time."

Johnson's face would never qualify for a sun-tanning advertisement, but on this occasion, he displayed a pure white coloring that perhaps no one but his mother had seen in his lifetime. "Alright. I did have an affair going with her."

"Of course," said Fraser.

"It started off harmlessly. We played in plenty of tournaments together. She started to find excuses for physical contact. She'd touch me, push a hip or a breast against me. When we had a good game — and we had lots of good ones — she'd get more aggressive. We went to her hotel room one afternoon after a session and she announced she was going to have a bath. She undressed and I... I couldn't help it. I fell for her. After that, it took no excuse at all to get us going. She was beautiful."

"Harry never caught on?"

"We were very careful. Harry was always doing his own thing. He chased women all the time. I'm sure he must have known about Louise and me. I doubt that he cared. He never let on, anyway."

"And you were friends right up to the time she disappeared?" asked Fraser.

"Pretty much."

"Pretty much means Louise could be a little tough to be with?" asked Fraser.

"What do you mean?"

"Word has it that she got a little arrogant. She treated you more like a servant than a partner."

"You mean toward the end?"

"Whatever," said Fraser.

"I suppose you're right. She was a good average player and we worked on our system a lot. I mean I taught her all she ever knew about bidding. I wrote out the whole system for her, what every bid meant. I coached her on the play, too. She didn't ever learn anything from Harry." Johnson hesitated.

"And," coaxed Fraser.

"And toward the end, she got to thinking she was really good, that she had some natural talent for the game. She didn't, damn it. No flair at all. She could handle simple, repetitive situations, but anything that required a little imagination was way beyond her." He paused again.

After a few moments of silence, Fraser said, "Go on."

"Well, she seemed to acquire this streak of arrogance. She belittled everything we did. Even sex. I guess Harry is hung like an elephant. She started to make jokes about that. I never went after her. I just took what she offered. And in our games, she became a total result analyst. If I made a wrong decision, any hairline decision on a bid or play that went sour, she started to bluster about it. It got so I could hardly stand playing with her any more."

"Yet she left you the business in her will," said Fraser.

"Yes. If you go back several years, there was a time when we were getting along particularly well. We won events in several regionals. It seemed that all we had to do was show up and we'd win two or three events. Or maybe place in a couple and win one. She really came on to me during that time. Asked if there was anything she could do. Finally, I said yes. I asked her to leave me a piece of the business. I built the damned business for Harry anyway. He was a smart guy in a lot of ways, but he didn't know his arse from his elbow when it came to investing. He had these friends who were clients. Harry put them into portfolios that made a small amount for the clients and he scooped off a couple of percent a year. They stuck with him because they were good friends. Louise had buckets of money and the Laches didn't need his business to live on. This operation was just pocket change to her. So I asked Louise to leave me the business when Harry retired. She owned it. Harry didn't put a penny into it. He didn't have a penny to put in. So she agreed to leave it all to me in her will, or when Harry retired, to pass it on to me. I think she forgot about the whole deal after she signed the papers. She never spoke of it again, and never threatened to revoke it at any time."

"Rumor has it that you had your problems with Harry as well."

"Harry hired me when I graduated. He gave me the only job I've ever had. I respect that. But when Louise went after me and I caved in, I guess Harry got wind of it and his attitude towards me cooled. Maybe froze is a better word. The warmth in our relationship just disappeared. I may not have had much use for Harry personally or as a businessman, but he did give me a job. When you graduate and don't have a penny in your pocket, you wonder what in hell comes next. Then when someone shows up and offers you a job at a salary way more than your father ever earned, you have to have some feeling of gratitude towards the guy."

"So after a few years with Harry, you came out well ahead of the game," said Fraser.

"I never thought of it that way. I figured that I built the business during the time I was here into a really profitable little operation. I'm not rich, for God's sake. Look at some of my classmates who went to work for the brokers in New York. They're multi-millionaires now. I'm comfortable, but not on that scale."

"I guess you weren't sorry to see the Laches disappear from the scene?"

"Yes and no. What are you insinuating? You think I wished this on them? Disappearance and then murder? Don't even think it. Sure, I had problems with both of them, but I owed them a lot, too."

"You took over the business."

"True, but Harry paid me well before that."

"You got rid of a nagging bridge partner."

"You can look at it that way if you choose."

"Okay," said Fraser. "I'm finished here for now. Thanks for your cooperation."

— —

Fraser made contact with Louise Lache's niece, a Shirley Palmer, from Madison, Wisconsin. He informed her that he was investigating the murders of her aunt and uncle and inquired whether she had time for an extensive phone interview. She agreed and told him a time when she would be available.

He called her back late on Monday morning after obtaining a recent photo of her from the Laches' funeral. A shy, willowy peroxide blonde dressed in a green suede suit stood at the gravesides, flowers strewn near her feet. Fraser judged her to be in her early forties at most.

"Sorry to bother you," said Fraser.

"If you'd been in town last week, we could have saved ourselves a phone call. I was there last week to arrange the funeral," said Shirley, in a soft, musical voice that Fraser found a delight to listen to. "One has to be ready for these affairs. I wondered for a long time what happened to Aunt Louise. They've been gone for so long now. I had a feeling that something terrible had happened."

Fraser related the murder of the Hills over the weekend.

"My goodness. The town is becoming a violent place."

"Yes. It's really been shaken up. Do you know your way around the town?"

"I was there a lot in happier times. But, yes, I do know the town. Not that I don't like Erieville, but apart from the funeral, there's nothing for me to do there."

"We have a few questions for you, of course."

"I expect so."

"You were the sole beneficiary in the Lache will?"

"So I understand. That's apart from the business. Aunt Louise left it to Ron, and that was fair. She was the only family I had left. Everyone else is gone. I ended up with most of the family money."

"The property on Wellesley Island must have been valuable."

"Oh yes. I had no need for the money, but no one turns down a windfall."

"You kept the property for quite a while."

"I wasn't sure what to do with it. I finally decided that I would never use the property at all, so I put in on the market. Our lakes in Wisconsin are the nicest in the country. I don't need two summer places to look after."

"Have you met Ron and Beth?"

"A few times. We've always been on good terms."

"Did you know that your uncle Harry had a child with Beth?"

He heard a muffled sound of surprise from her end of the phone.

"Heavens, no."

"That's the story. There was no provision in the will for the child. You might want to talk to Beth about it."

"I surely will."

"Now, let's go back to your aunt and uncle. Do you have any thoughts on who might have had something against them?"

"No. Not at all. Our gatherings were always pleasant. I can't stand bickering, and Aunt Louise understood that. She would never invite me unless she had a friendly group to join us."

Fraser put down the phone, thinking that this wealthy young lady lacked the motive and the temperament to have had anything to do with the murder of her relatives.

— —

The officers met later that day at the motel to compare notes.

Stan said, "We ought to download my pictures of the tire tracks and email them to your contacts in Albany. They may be able to tell us something. I have the cable we need to go straight from the camera to the computer."

"I thought you found out everything you need from your tire dealer," said Fraser.

"I have a whole lot of possibilities. I'd like to boil them down to a conclusion. The forensic pros can do that better than the amateurs I've been talking to," said Stan. "Shouldn't be a whole lot of work."

Fraser gave in to his continuing persistence and Stan connected his camera to the computer to set up a file. He sent the pictures in an email along with a note requesting priority service. Dot Lamant phoned a few hours later.

"I've got a pretty good idea of the type of each of your tires," she said. "One is from an all-season tread, a good size. The wear looks about maybe forty, fifty thousand miles. That's just a guess. If it's close, it would make the car two or three years old. The other one looks like a winter tire. It's from a full-size car as well. It's not nearly as clear, and it's barely worn. I'd say eight to ten thousand miles at most. That might make the tires less than a year old. That would depend on how much switching they did between winter and summer. Then there's a third tire in the photos. It's a tread from a smaller car, a generic tread from a replacement type that you pick up at a tire dealer."

Stan interrupted her. "I wonder if one of those is from the Hill's car. They owned a new-looking Buick Park Avenue."

"That might fit," said Dot. "It looks like a Bridgestone tread and GM use them a lot. You'll have to match up that information with actual vehicles. If you want to track down your known vehicles and send me photos of their tire treads, I'll run a comparison. They're not as useful as fingerprints, but I might be able to help narrow your possibilities down."

"Thanks, Dot," said Stan. "I'll get going on that."

Stan passed the information on to Fraser and Macvey.

"We're looking for fairly new and fairly old tires," said Piper. "Maybe from the island, maybe not. I can check with the local service stations to see if I get a lead on either of them. I'm going to take a look at the Hill's Buick before I do anything else. It's still right here on the property. Then I'll be able to eliminate one set of tracks and focus on the other. I'd like to do some more checking in Erieville. It'll be a real fluke if we come up with something, but you never know," he said.

Fraser said, "We don't want to go chasing our tail."

Stan persisted. "I'll focus on the vehicles of the people who were close to the Laches. That's not a big number. I can grab pictures of Johnson's tires and Lugner's. Maybe Beth's. I'll get Gehl's and Lucy's while I'm at it. That covers the whole territory, and it won't take long. I'll bet a nickel that at least one of the vehicles is from the island. It wouldn't surprise me if someone dropped over for a look and took off when they saw the bodies. The other one could be the tracks of the murderer. Who knows?"

"Have we had any curiosity seekers looking around?" Fraser asked.

"A couple of cars slowed down, but that's about it," Brad said.

"I guess there aren't that many people around here at this time of year. Tourists haven't started to come yet."

"Good thing, too," said Stan. "We don't need spectators for this kind of work."

Stan took his leave and headed back to the Hills' place to capture the details of the tires on each wheel of the Buick.

CHAPTER 12

Fraser was about to drop into Cameron's office late Monday afternoon. He had mixed feelings about terminating the investigation. He and Cameron were well aware of the agreement that had been struck between Cameron and Gordon Bryder, including the condition that at the end of two weeks Fraser would return to his home unit near Buffalo. That agreement had been made when there were two murders involved, and the case had been dormant for four years. Now, four murders were involved, and two of them had happened just recently. Suddenly, the case had been transformed from cold to red hot. How could he leave? His attitude had changed. He wanted to stay on the case until he wrapped it up. He pondered how to cover this to best advantage as he headed for Cameron's office.

When his cell phone buzzed in his pocket, he considered letting it go and listening to the message after he finished with Cameron. Finally, after three buzzes, he pulled the phone out and answered it.

"Art?" asked a voice.

"Speaking."

"This is Mike Eppler. How's your case going?"

"Terrible. We're thinking of wrapping it up."

"I've got something that may help. We located your Cadillac."

"What do you mean my Cadillac?"

"Remember you asked me to help look for a '98 Caddie? We found it."

"You found it! I can't believe this," said Fraser, stunned by the news. Possibilities flooded his mind.

"Somebody parked it in an old barn outside the town of Fort Meade, a bit south of Orlando. There's a property there; it's maybe twenty acres of mostly swamp. The hurricane that went through there last fall blew the barn down. It was a rickety old building ready to fall anyway. There she was. Looked like she was brand new. Nobody paid any attention. When we got the vehicle registration numbers, they matched up with the ones you gave me. The suitcases in the trunk were like new. All their personal stuff was in there, untouched over the last four years."

"That's fantastic. Who owns the barn?"

"They're tracking all that down. You ought to pay a visit to Fort Meade, or maybe send one of your guys."

"This might break the case. Can you send me the details?"

"I'll send everything by email — the exact location, and your contact down there. They're holding the car for you at the station in Fort Meade."

"Sensational, Mike. I'm just heading in to see Cameron. I'll bring him up to date and then make arrangements to get somebody down to Fort Meade right away."

Fraser shuddered to think that he had almost turned the ringer off on his cell phone. By the time he entered Cameron's office, his mood had picked up considerably. Cameron noticed it at once.

"Is there a new spring in the man's step?" Cameron asked.

Fraser related the call from Eppler and what they needed to do. "Someone has to get down to Fort Meade. I'm going to send Stan as soon as he can get a flight."

"Hmm," said Cameron. "I'd like to see Macvey going. Tell you why. He's a regular officer and we can easily assign him. Piper is a part-timer, a retiree. If anything happens, I have no liability insurance to cover him. Macvey is covered. Same deal as you got after you were wounded. It'll be much cleaner if we send Brad."

Fraser, in a fit of pique at being over-ruled on a simple decision, made a careless comment. "Brad will stagger his way around down there. I hope he doesn't run into any turkeys."

"That's not a smart way to talk about a colleague. In any case, if he does, you're covered."

Fraser left, called Brad and Stan on their cell phones and checked the office computer to get his email message from Mike Eppler. The three detectives met in a small conference room in the Jefferson county police headquarters. Fraser passed on the news about the Lache car. "Someone has to go down there to make contact with the Fort Meade police and arrange to have the car shipped here," said Fraser. "Brad, we've elected you for the job."

Macvey was obviously pleased with this news. "I need to check with Sophie," he blurted.

"Henpecked and not even married," joked Stan.

"They're expecting you pronto," said Fraser.

"I guess I can make it," said Macvey. "Maybe I can get a round of golf in there.

I know a course down in Orlando that's just like Saint Andrews. I mean they've got one hole just like Saint Andrews."

"Tell us about it," said Fraser, without enthusiasm.

"The seventeenth hole is just like the road hole at Saint Andrews. The only difference is you hit over a sewage treatment plant instead of a hotel. Course, if the wind is blowing the wrong way--"

"Do you think there'll be anything left of the course after the hurricane?" said Stan, grinning.

"I have no idea. The greens are like velvet, I know that much."

"If you like brown velvet," smirked Stan. "How do you know so much about Saint Andrews?"

"That's where my grandfather is from. I've been there a couple of times."

Fraser interrupted. "Okay. We'll have to get you plane tickets to Orlando and you can rent a car at the airport there. Fort Meade is a little south. Remember, you're down there on business, not a tourist junket. The main order of business is to arrange for the car to be shipped up here to Erieville. I don't even know if it's drivable. But we need it here as part of our evidence. It would help greatly if we could lift some fingerprints from the vehicle. You need to make friends with your contact down there and go over the car thoroughly. You're going to be a busy boy and you can't go running off entertaining yourself."

"Fine. I just thought if there was time--"

"There isn't," snapped Fraser. "We may have a big break in our case, just when it looked like it was drying up, and nobody, including you, I hope, wants to see us wasting time."

"He'll be okay," said Stan. "You can't blame a man for trying to work in a little golf."

Fraser took out the note he had received from Eppler and dialed a number in Fort Meade. He asked for Sergeant Bill Wooler and was connected quickly. Wooler confirmed that the Cadillac they looked for was in the Fort Meade compound, and that he would be pleased to have a visit from Brad Macvey as soon as flight arrangements could be made. Macvey would be down on Tuesday and in Wooler's office shortly after lunch. Fraser mentioned that he was hoping that Macvey could return late Tuesday evening.

Wooler said, "I better pick him up at Orlando. That would save him a lot of time. I can drop him off at night as well. You need a native guide to navigate our backwoods roads down here."

"That would be terrific. We owe you one," responded Fraser.

They closed the conversation after Wooler said they did not yet know who owned the property where the car had been found. He promised to look into the matter right away.

"There's a funny thing about the tire tracks," said Stan, when he and Fraser were alone. "The one tread is definitely a Goodyear Eagle. As for the other two, Lucy Dinde and Beth both drive Intrepids, Johnson has a Concorde, Lugner has a Three Hundred. The tracks are specific to those models."

"They must all be Chrysler shareholders," chuckled Fraser.

"I sent photos of all the tires to Dot in Albany. She compared them to the tracks on the lawn. According to her, there's no way to tell the difference between them. I find that hard to believe. There must be some mark on those tires that would make one different from the other."

"Why don't we stop wasting time," barked Fraser. "If Dot Lamant can't find a difference, what makes you think you can?"

"All right," said a subdued Stan. "But how about I get soil samples from each of the cars and send them off to Albany? They might be able to work out if one of them has been at the Hill place."

"Go ahead," said Fraser curtly.

CHAPTER 13

On Tuesday night Macvey returned from his car-hunting expedition in Florida, relaxed and much the happier for a bit of sun. After leaving Syracuse airport, he stopped at Sophie's apartment for a brief but energetic rendezvous, and rose early on Wednesday to drive to Erieville to meet his colleagues. Stan and Fraser were waiting in the Erieville police station room, idly chatting about the case, especially the way things were picking up with the two new leads they had uncovered.

"What a rush," said Brad. "No time for a man to do anything. I just ran from one place to the next. No direct flights. I had to make a connection in Washington both ways."

"How was the car?" asked Fraser.

"The Caddie is fine. Perfect, in fact. It has a couple of scratches from the barn falling down, but the thing looks almost new."

"It's on its way here?"

"Wooler said to figure on three days. He'll try to get it here sooner, but the driver has to sleep."

"We have no choice anyway."

"I hope we get some decent prints from it," said Stan.

"I went over the whole thing," said Macvey. "The inside anyway. Their forensic guy helped me. We took digital pictures of all the areas where we got positive signs from the dusting. I brought them with me."

"Good," said Fraser. "Let's send them to our man in Albany to compare them with what we have on file. If we're lucky, we'll find more than just Lache prints."

"I could run them down to Albany," volunteered Stan. "I'll take the soil samples along too."

"You're going to have to go like hell to collect soil samples and get to Albany in time to accomplish anything," said Fraser.

"I already got 'em," grinned Piper. "Four little ziplock bags full of dirt."

Fraser laughed. "Well, go ahead. If you're ready to head out now, you might as well. That'll save us time in the long run."

Fraser decided that they would start the second round of interviews with Gehl. The best way to get Gehl talking would be to have him at his ease, and it worked out well that he and Brad would be the ones making the call.

Brad doesn't carry any airs, thought Fraser. *Gehl seems to relax with him. They have a connection from a couple of generations ago. Besides, nobody else can handle the dogs up there.*

Fraser and Macvey left the station and drove through a foggy patch on Highway 81 to the island. They arrived at Gehl's place about eleven. Macvey did his usual trick with the dogs and when Gehl opened the door, dressed in his usual garb, he gave the officers a genuine welcome. Fraser wondered how to start an interview with a man they were about to confront as a liar. He was pleased when Macvey broke the ice and inquired about Gehl's relationship with Lucy.

"We've known each other quite a while," said Gehl. "I've been here nearly thirty-five years now and she moved in here at least twenty years ago."

"How come you never moved in together?" asked Macvey.

Fraser was sure this would cause a mild explosion, but Gehl chuckled. Evidently Macvey had his man figured out. "I mentioned it a couple of times. Even tried it. It didn't work out. We was incombustible."

"You mean incompatible?" asked Macvey.

"No. I mean incombustible. No point having a woman around if you can't light a fire." Macvey joined in the laughter as Gehl threw his head back and chuckled more loudly than ever, exposing two rows of unevenly yellowed teeth.

"You like her well enough, apart from that?" continued Macvey.

"Oh yeah. We get along fine. She liked Harry better than me anyway. She liked Hill too. I was in third place most of the time. I never got along with Hill. Like I told you before, he was a hard man to pry money out of. He nickled and dimed me every time I went to collect. But Lucy seemed to hit it off okay with him."

Fraser was about to say that that was not what he had told them earlier, but Macvey kept the conversation moving and did not break the rapport.

"You mean Lucy had it going with Lache and Hill?"

"Not at the same time. She and Lache went at it pretty good for a while and then something happened and she got mad. She never went over there again. But Hill was always sniffing around, and when she got mad at Lache, she started to pay attention to Hill instead. That really pissed me off, too. I had no use for Hill and there she was cozying up to him. I tried to tell her what kind of guy he was, but she didn't care."

"Did this affair with Hill go on for long?" asked Macvey.

"It cooled off after the Laches disappeared. I'm not sure why. I guess the Hills stopped coming up here as much, or maybe they spent more time together when there was no Lache party going on. Everything that happened around here had to do with the Laches. They were the sparkplugs of the group. They had all kinds of people up here, playing cards, golf, you name it. Hill would take them out on his boat every now and then. That was all he did. The visitors stayed at the Lache place. They had enough bedrooms to run a hotel."

Fraser had been letting Macvey take the lead in the conversation. Now he wanted to nudge it towards the day the Hills were murdered and probe Gehl's memory of that incident more deeply. He spoke for the first time since they had sat down in Gehl's kitchen. "I've had stronger coffee," he said with a smile. "I just can't remember when."

"With the price of coffee, it doesn't pay to make a brew nobody can taste. Might as well drink tea."

"True," agreed Fraser. "Now, going back to the Hills. They were pretty good friends of the Laches?"

"Oh yeah. They first came up here in the mid eighties. I guess they fell in love with the place. That happens, you know. That big old river is nice. Built-in air conditioning. Keeps it cool all summer. They like to play golf. I guess they figured they'd make plenty of friends here. They came back later in the summer and made a serious search for a property. Bob found one — six acres, on the water, close to the public dock where he could anchor his boat. The house was well looked after and he closed the deal pretty smartly. Didn't horse around."

"And the property was right next door to the Laches," said Fraser.

"Oh yeah. It didn't take long for them to get acquainted. They was goin' back and forth a lot. Playin' golf and cards all the time."

"When the Hills came up last weekend, did Hill call on Lucy? They couldn't have been here long before they were murdered."

"I figure they got here on Friday night. They were here all day Saturday. She come over to say hello; he didn't. We had so many falling outs, he wouldn't come near my place. But she's a classy woman. I suppose they dropped in on Lucy. Don't see why not."

"And you didn't notice anything strange on Saturday at all?" asked Fraser.

"I'm trying to think," said Gehl. "What was I doing Saturday? Had coffee in the morning. Said hello to Mrs. Hill just before lunch. Did a few jobs in the afternoon. Went to town to get some groceries."

"Did you pass any cars on the way to town?" asked Macvey.

"Pass cars?" snorted Gehl. "'Course I passed cars. When you head down Highway 81, you pass a million cars."

"How about on the island roads?" asked Fraser.

"Island roads? How in hell am I supposed to remember that? Let me think." Gehl paused for a few moments, scratched himself in several places, rubbed his nose, started to mutter, and then stopped. "Yeah," he continued. "I did see a couple of cars on the way back from 81. I can't tell them apart."

"Do you remember the colors?" asked Fraser.

"Colors? Brown. Light brown. Sort of tan. Gold you might say. Both of them. Yeah. That was funny. Two cars the same color. Both a sort of gold. Nice color."

"You didn't see anyone you recognized in the cars?"

"No. When I drive, I look at the road, not at people. Besides, I had things to do."

"And around the house, did you see anyone or anything during the day?"

"I already told you that. Come to think of it, there was a woman in one of the cars. Blonde hair. Definitely. I remember now."

"Which car?" asked Fraser.

"I told you I can't tell them apart."

"Let's go back to '99," said Fraser. "Did the Hills do or say anything that might indicate they knew something? I think their deaths are somehow related to the Lache murder."

"'99 again," said Gehl. "Well, they were up here all right. There was one day they come over and Hill asked me if I had seen the Laches. I knew they were heading south somewhere to play cards and I didn't figure to see them for a couple of weeks. Harry usually paid me off a little ahead when he was traveling. He didn't do that this time. Said he'd get caught up as soon as he came back. Hill was sure he'd seen the Lache car that night, but that was impossible. Harry told me they were leaving for sure the day before. He had no plans to come up here. Hill said Harry's yard was a big mess. Got chewed up when the Caddie roared out at one hell of a clip. Didn't make any sense. I went over the next day and sure enough the lawn was full of deep ruts. I raked it up for them."

"Okay," said Fraser, as he got up to leave. "Thanks for your help. We'll be back for more, I'm sure. Thanks for the coffee."

Fraser and Macvey took their leave and headed for Lucy Dinde's place. "I'm not sure we made any progress," said Fraser. "But we have another lead to track down."

"Lots of tracking. I wonder what Lucy has for us."

"Let's hope it's not a shovel," said Fraser slyly.

They pulled into Lucy's yard and spotted her, as they always had, performing a vigorous outdoor task. This time she was repairing her fence, lugging cedar rails to lay between sets of posts in the ground.

"Don't get in the way of one of those if she swings around," advised Fraser.

"And don't turn your backside on her," counseled Macvey. "Hi, Lucy," he shouted, careful to advertise his presence from a distance.

Lucy did swing her rail around, but the officers were safely out of reach. She rested her load, greeted the officers and asked what they wanted.

"Another little talk," said Macvey. "We haven't wrapped this case up yet."

"I've told you everything I know already. Come on in. Let's get it over with."

She led the officers into her kitchen, pointed out some chairs and made some coffee.

"Everybody drinks coffee around here by the gallon," remarked Fraser.

"You don't have to have any if you don't like it. You want a beer or a glass of water?"

"Coffee is fine. I've already had three cups. I should be sharp for the rest of the day."

"Lucy, I've been hearing stories about you," said Brad. "I hear you and Harry had a thing going."

"Where would you hear a thing like that? I hated the bugger. Oh yeah, he'd come sniffing around looking for it, and I let him in some times, but I told you, he cheated me at cards and I had nothing to do with him after that."

"You never had anything to do with either of the Laches after that?"

"Louise was nice enough, but she never had much use for me. Not that she bothered me, but she didn't want to be good friends or anything."

"I guess that's natural if you and Harry were friendly."

Lucy opened her mouth at this, as if about to say something. Then she thought better of it and laughed. "Yeah. I know what you mean. Believe me, I never went after Harry. He came after me. Still, I could see why that would bother her."

"I understand Mister Hill came calling too," said Brad.

"You're gonna think I'm a regular neighborhood madam," said Lucy. "That's not it at all. I'm a widow, all alone here. If a man comes along every now and then, that's my business."

"We understand," said Fraser. "We're not judging you. We have a murder to solve and we need to get the facts straight. Two men were murdered who were close to you and you had affairs with both of them."

Lucy looked as if she were about to cry, but just for a moment. She recovered her composure quickly and said, "Okay, boys. What do you want?"

"We need you to open up, Lucy," Fraser said. "When the Hills came up here, did you notice anything happening in their yard? Any cars or people? Did anyone go onto their property?"

"Honestly, I didn't see a thing all day long. I spend a lot of time in my kitchen and I can't see their front yard from here."

"Did you hear anything?" asked Macvey.

"It's pretty quiet up here, except for the wind, animals, the odd car going by."

"There was nothing that stood out?" asked Fraser.

"Not a thing," said Lucy.

"Let's go back to the time when the Laches were still alive. Can you tell us any more about that?" asked Fraser.

"What do you want to know? The weather? My garden?" Lucy laughed at the question.

"We need to know about people who came up here, and who might have had a motive for the murder. You were mad at Harry yourself. Was there anyone else? Then the Hills were killed just when they got here for a holiday. Did they know something that could incriminate the Lache killer? We need to track down the background information. Something is missing. People either lie or they don't tell us everything. People like you."

"Just a minute. I don't fancy people telling me I'm lying."

"You certainly didn't tell us everything," said Fraser.

"Okay, but I'm not a mind reader. You need to let me in on what you want to know."

"We need to know as much as possible about who came up here. Tell us about the bridge games. Who was here and how did people get along? Surely you know that kind of thing."

"I'm not a busybody. I told you all the people that were here when I used to play."

"Anybody else?" asked Fraser.

"Yes. There was a girl. She looked like Jayne Mansfield. Her boobs were bigger than mine. She was slim to boot. I could see why Harry would pant after her. He brought her up here occasionally."

"Now that's interesting. When did she come up?"

"It was only for a couple of summers. Mostly on Wednesdays in the afternoons. She would come up, stay the afternoon, and then take off. She always had her own car. I never saw her drive with Harry. She wasn't in the bridge group. I never saw her play, anyway. Not when I used to play."

"Did anyone else come with them?"

"Not that I saw. She didn't come every Wednesday, either. I just happened to notice, a couple of weeks in a row, that she came up on a Wednesday afternoon. After that, I started to watch for her and she was here some times and not others."

"Was she ever around the same time as the Hills?"

"Not that I remember. The Hills were mostly weekend visitors. They came up on holiday weekends. Occasionally, they'd come for a whole week. It seemed they came when Laches were here. They probably arranged their times together."

"So Harry had a little visit with Beth every so often," said Fraser, looking at Macvey.

"Who's Beth?" asked Lucy.

"There's a girl who works in Lache's office. She did then and she still does. She happens to fit your description perfectly."

"I didn't know I described anyone," said Lucy.

"'Jayne Mansfield' did it," said Brad, smiling.

"Oh."

"Were the Hills popular?" asked Fraser, resuming his role as interrogator.

"I always liked them. I don't remember them having enemies. Nobody who'd want to kill them anyway."

"Your neighbor didn't like them much."

"Who? Gehl? He's just grumpy. They had an argument once over how much Hill owed him for some work. That cooled them off, but they still got along. Aside from that, Bob was a straight player. He leveled things with Lache."

"What do you mean 'leveled'?"

"He won money off Lache playing cards. Not too many people can say that." Fraser scratched his head.

"Okay, thanks Lucy. If you can't think of anything else to add about last Saturday, we'll be on our way."

"I wish I could be more help. I'll be in touch if I think of anything."

The officers thanked Lucy for the coffee and left. As they were getting into Macvey's car, Fraser's cell phone rang. It was Stan calling from Albany.

"We got the fingerprint analysis results. Lache prints, mainly. Both Mister and Missus show up. There are two others there that we don't have on file. We'll have to find a way to get more if we're going to get anywhere with prints."

"That shouldn't be too hard."

"Joe here says if we get good ink prints, we can scan them and email them to him. He can let us know right away about any matches."

"Good going. Brad and I will work out a way to get prints. Our best bet is to be up front and just ask everyone. If anyone balks, they'll have a reason. We can collect them this afternoon."

"Sounds good. They're still working on the soil samples. They'll take a while longer. We'll have them tomorrow night, he says."

"Okay. Are you heading back right now?"

"I'm in my car. I'll be in Erieville in three hours."

"Four," said Fraser, knowing how fast Stan would have to drive to get there in hours.

"ee," repeated Stan, and hung up.

"You're a fingerprint expert, aren't you?" Fraser asked Brad.

"I did some at Fort Meade on the Caddie. I'm not an expert," said Brad, who was not in love with messy, detailed procedures. "Everybody gets dirty."

"Nothing to it," scoffed Fraser. "We'll get Lucy and Gehl before we head back and then round up everyone in Erieville. You can handle the explanations to the people here and I'll do the same when we get to the Erieville crowd."

"What am I supposed to say? You're under suspicion of murder and we need to check you out?"

"If you like. Or you might just say we have some important fingerprints on file. We need to compare them with others connected to the case, clearing most."

"Okay. Do you have a kit with you?"

"Always."

The officers surprised Lucy when they returned to her house so soon. Macvey informed her that they needed to take some fingerprints. "Don't worry. The ink will come off easy. You're not under suspicion, not yet anyway. We have no prints yet."

Lucy responded, "I like the way you say not yet. Try getting more coffee out of me."

"Just hold your hand out, left first."

Lucy cocked an eyebrow at the young officer. If she had any thoughts of resisting, the offer of physical contact overcame any objection and she complied readily. When she had completed a full set of prints, she grasped Brad's cheeks with both hands and kissed him. His normally handsome, tanned face was now a mess of blushing red and fingerprint black.

"Oh, dear. I've gone and messed you all up. Come on into the bathroom and I'll get you cleaned up."

Brad could not see how strange he looked, but he certainly felt that something was not right. He let her lead him to the bathroom. The reflection in the mirror proved that something, indeed, was not right, but he remained passive as Lucy applied soap and water with a rough wash cloth. She finished him off with an even rougher towel. A great deal of skin came off with the ink and Brad's face was redder than ever by the time she had finished her cleaning process.

"Poor dear," said Lucy as she gave Brad another kiss and sent the officers on their way.

Gehl's dogs must have sensed that something was out of the ordinary. Brad found it impossible to quiet them when he got out of the car and it took a minute of Gehl's profanity to do the job. Gehl himself proved to be more of a problem than Lucy, but Macvey's homespun style seemed to overcome his resistance. He went along with the request. Thankfully, he did not try to kiss any of the officers when the fingerprinting was finished. He uttered a few oaths and headed for the bathroom.

On the drive to Erieville, Fraser said, "You're quite a hit with Lucy."

Brad blushed and muttered. "She gives out a little more information every time we talk to her. It would kill her to tell us everything she knows at once."

They arrived in Erieville just before noon and decided to call on Lugner first. The old man was impatient about the whole process and grumbled about having to spend an hour cleaning up. Fraser broached the subject of interviewing Jason.

"What in hell for?" demanded Lugner.

"He was around at the time of the death of the Laches," answered Fraser. "Anybody who might have some relevant facts for us has to be interviewed."

"I don't see you have any reason to bother the kid. I can vouch for him."

"He's hardly a kid, Mr. Lugner. Anyway, that's beside the point. We wouldn't be doing our job if we didn't follow every lead we have. I can get a court order if I have to."

"I've bent over backwards to help you so far. You insult me every possible way. First you come in and insist on my damned fingerprints and then you won't take my word on the young man's character. That's a hell of a way to reward coopera-tion."

Fraser saw that the conversation was getting nowhere and cut it off. "We have others to fingerprint today. I'll call you about talking to Jason."

Beth was her normal attractive, grim, unsmiling self, and Johnson was submis-sive as usual. On the whole, dealing with these folks was easier than dealing with the islanders. They were able to scan and send the information to Albany by early afternoon.

Fraser asked the pair if they could add anything to their previous statements about the Hills. Beth surprised them both with useful information. "Yes. I remem-ber a strange call from Mr. Hill around the time Mr. and Mrs. Lache were on their way to San Antonio. He asked about them, thinking he saw their car on Wellesley

Island the night before. He was so positive about it. I told him about the trip and that he couldn't possibly have seen their car. I never heard anything more about it."

Stan, true to his forecast of a three-hour trip, showed up late in the afternoon. "Feels like we're getting somewhere now," he said.

"We ought to wrap it up this year sometime," remarked Macvey.

"We'll have some fingerprint data that may or may not help. How we tie that all together with motive, opportunity, murder weapon and all the rest remains to be seen," cautioned Fraser. "We don't even have a prime suspect yet."

"It bothers me though, that we seem to osculate all the time," Brad said.

"You mean oscillate?" asked Stan.

"No. I mean go back and forth. One step forward and a couple back. Like a pendulum," explained Macvey. "In relation to the case. Beth seems like a nice young lady, and we find she's had a kid by Lache. Lucy was giving it to Lache and then she gets mad at him and they don't see each other again. Old man Lugner never admits to any problem between himself and the Laches, and you find out they fought every time they sat down. Then our friend Johnson has something going with Mrs. Lache. These characters are all twisted around one another somehow. Nobody wants to admit anything. We try to dig deep, but every time we talk to someone, the story changes."

Fraser mulled over the fragments they had heard over the past few days, where each story contradicted the previous one. "Yes. Appearances showed they were all good friends, yet we find a ton of conflicts below the surface. What did the Hills know that got them killed?"

"If we find that, we've solved the case," said Macvey.

"No kidding," said Stan. "I thought your second round of questions was going to sort all this out."

"It just gave us a different version," said Fraser. "The car information may be a big break. When Albany gives us the word on the fingerprints, we'll have a case."

"I say follow the motive," said Stan. "Johnson became a millionaire, or close to it, when the Laches died. That's a hell of an incentive."

"All of the people we've talked to so far have a motive," said Fraser. "Go down the list. They all had something against one of the Laches. The Hills' deaths, that must be the key to the whole thing. Nobody had anything against them, except maybe old man Gehl, and his problem was pretty small. The Hills must have known facts that the Laches' killer didn't want to surface. They knew or maybe saw something important."

"Or maybe the murderer just *thought* they saw or knew something significant," added Macvey.

"True," conceded Stan. "But what could they have seen? And how could the murderer have come to the conclusion that they were dangerous? They must have seen someone digging, or a car arriving or leaving, something like that that would lead directly to the murderer."

"Whatever the Hills saw or heard was a minor thing at the time, but that all changed once the bodies were dug up," said Macvey.

"What could have changed?" asked Stan.

"We need to look at the psychology at work here," Fraser said, "as well as at the bare facts. Let's say that the killer deals with the Laches, dumps the bodies in a vehicle, drives up here after dark, buries the bodies in the yard and takes off back to Erieville. If the Hills spotted the driver of the Lache car the night of the murder, and according to Beth they must have, that fact in itself would be of little consequence. The only thing of significance is whether the murderer believed he, or she, had been recognized. Thinking you were spotted by someone who could identify you would make the sighting really important, but not until the murder had been established. There was no need to panic, because at the time of the Lache murder and for the next four years, only one person knew there had even been a murder. The sighting only became crucial when the Lache bodies were dug up and the murder was proven. The killer would now have every reason to think the Hills could finger him."

"One of the Hills might have seen the body bags being moved around. Or maybe the murderer ran out of gas and had to get some from the Hills," Macvey said.

"I can't believe anyone would be dumb enough to ask a neighbor for gas after burying a couple of bodies," said Stan.

"There might be something to Brad's idea of a need for gas," Fraser said.

"Doesn't matter how smart you are. If your car is out of gas you won't go any-where. Maybe the murdered went to a gas station and encountered the Hills there where the light was good enough for them to recognize him."

"Maybe," said Macvey. "And now, four years later, the only possible witnesses are the Hills, and they gotta go."

"Exactly," said Fraser.

After refreshing their coffee, they resumed their seats around the table in the sparse office quarters that were beginning to feel like home.

"I've been thinking that we ought to ask the folks at the bridge to the island if they have any video camera records of cars going back and forth" said Macvey.

"From four years ago? I doubt it," said Stan.

"I'm talking about this past weekend," snapped Brad. "Four years ago is ancient history now. The way I see it, we're pretty sure the bodies were trucked around in the Lache Cadillac. The tapes wouldn't show who was driving. They'd just show us the license plate. But from this Saturday's tapes, we ought to be able to figure who came across, and maybe spot our killer's plates."

Stan grumbled agreement.

"Another thing," said Macvey. "We might have a better chance of getting infor-mation by checking with operators of the gas stations right by the bridge. There's one on the island and two on the mainland, close to the bridge. If any of them old hands who happened to be around at the time, they might remember something. Especially if there was anything unusual going on. A thunderstorm, or maybe an accident."

"That won't take long and it's certainly worth doing," agreed Fraser. "While we're at it, it wouldn't have had to be a gas station. He might have stopped at a convenience store or any place with toilet facilities. Someone somewhere might recall something. We have the exact date and we can bracket the time of the mur-der. Chances are the murderer drove onto the island during the day and drove home that night."

"There's a restaurant on the road to the Hills' place," said Macvey. "On top of the pro shop at the golf club. Somebody might have stopped there."

The officers agreed to split up and call on the establishments they noted. They would meet a few hours later. Fraser wanted to stay in Erieville, where he felt con-vinced the clues to the case resided. Macvey was enthusiastic about calling at the

Thousand Islands bridge office. He was sure they had some sort of video surveillance of vehicles crossing the bridge and hoped that their cameras had picked up something useful. It was a slim chance, but the potential payoff was too large to ignore. Fraser agreed that Stan should go with Brad and they went their separate ways.

Stan and Brad arrived at the bridge office, and Brad, taking the lead, introduced them to the two officials manning the desk. They revealed that they did have cameras working on a twenty-four hour basis, and that several years of records were stored in the office right at the bridge.

"The filing system's not perfect, though, boys. I'm very doubtful about the quality of the footage," said one of the men.

"Nobody has ever gone through these records," contributed the other. "We don't. We keep them here just in case. You can go through as much as you like. We don't have the manpower to go through all of them with you."

"This is a case of murder," Macvey reminded the official. "We've got to look into any lead we come across. We can look at the tapes, but we need one of you gentlemen to explain your setup."

"In that case, the best thing to do then is to come by after four-thirty. That's our regular quitting time and one of us can stay with you for a few hours and go through what we've got."

And pick up a few hours of overtime pay, thought Macvey. *Why not?*

"Are the records filed by date?" he asked.

"More or less. We pack up two films every shift and put them on the shelves. We try to get them in sequence. I hope they're all in order. That's all I can tell you. Like I said, nobody really looks at them after we put them on the shelf."

Brad agreed to return after four-thirty, thanked the men, and he and Stan left. The pair divided responsibilities for checking out service stations, restaurants and convenience stores. The process was time consuming and a long shot, and they both knew it. When they compared notes, they discovered that their findings were similar and, as they had suspected, fruitless. In all of the establishments, employee turnover was high and none of the current employees had been around as long as four years. They decided to head to Erieville and report to Fraser.

CHAPTER 14

Meanwhile, Fraser headed for Erieville, mentally planning his interview with Lugner as he drove. He had a passing thought that he would have been wiser to ask one of his colleagues to come along and could see that he was on his own in formulating the questions. Tape-recording the whole conversation would be necessary, even though that would be awkward with no one along for assistance. He rang the doorbell and Lugner appeared without delay, dressed in expensive, rumpled clothes, as usual. Fraser received a searching frown before Lugner invited him in.

"A state visit, is that what we have here? One interview and a pack of fingerprints don't do it?" He uttered a hollow laugh, turned slowly and launched his stiff six-foot-four frame towards a sitting room. "What's this all about?" he wanted to know.

"First, I told you I have to talk to your man, Jason Wong. I trust that he's around today. Otherwise, I'll have to ask him to come over to the station."

"He's not here, as it happens," said Lugner. "He's out of town for a few days."

"When do you expect him back?"

Lugner mumbled, "Tonight."

"Fine," said Fraser. "Could you tell him to come over to the station tomorrow morning?"

Lugner grunted assent.

"Now for the second item we have to discuss. We're double-checking the notes we made from earlier testimony. Matters are much more serious with two more murders on our hands. And we have some inconsistencies in our earlier testimony."

"Well, you won't find any inconsistencies in my statements," said Lugner.

"Good," said Fraser. "Tell us more about your relationship with Harry. I understand that you guys went at each other fairly often."

"Harry and I were good friends. I told you that. We played together for years."

"We all know how long you played together," Fraser snapped. "Let's get into the time when you and Harry didn't get along. I'd like to know how it happened and some details."

Lugner tilted his chin and paused for thought. He seemed about to speak a couple of times, then thought better of it. Finally, Lugner sighed and began to speak.

"Harry and I knew each other going back to the fifties. We were young bucks and we loved bridge. So did Louise. We played every chance we could. Living in a small place like Erieville, we had time on our hands. No long days commuting. Five minutes to work. Five minutes to the golf course. And we found lots of regional tournaments to go to. They started holding them in Canada years ago. They were close, easy for us to get to. We'd try and find one every month. Then Harry hired Ron Johnson and he became a partner for Louise. Harry and I got to play regularly. We had a ball. I guess it was too much of a good thing. We finally started to get on each other's nerves. You can only take so much of one person at the bridge table. Everyone makes mistakes, and if neither partner is open about his mistakes, you have no way of discussing how to get better. Harry and I got into a rut where we weren't improving. We couldn't get a logical discussion going about who was at fault for which mistake and what to do. That was the end of it. We should have quit then. Did we? Hell no. We kept on for years, going at each other like kids. I can see now it was as much my fault as his. We were both too old to develop new partnerships, so we kept playing with each other. Then Harry and Louise disappeared and the problem all of a sudden didn't exist any more. I haven't played much bridge since."

"Your friendship ended a long time ago," said Fraser.

"You can think of it that way."

"Let's get at some details. On the night of July 19, 1999, Harry and Louise were packing to go to San Antonio. As far as we can tell, that was the same night they disappeared. You must have been preparing to go yourself. You were planning to fly down?"

"Yes. We'd planned to meet in San Antonio. Ron and I were flying down. Not together. I was leaving on the Thursday morning. Ron was leaving later in the day. I always stayed in the tournament hotel. He booked into something cheaper. That night, let's see, I wasn't doing much of anything, as I recall. Harry and Louise always left a couple of days early. They would have packed on Monday and left Tuesday. They'd arrive Thursday night. I remember asking for them at the hotel desk in San Antonio when I got there. They hadn't checked in. Ron and I were supposed to play with them that night. He phoned Beth later on. Nobody knew anything about them."

"You didn't organize any other games?"

"We had everything arranged to play with the Laches. All ten days. I could never play with Johnson. We weren't on the same page. We hung around on Friday, asking around if they had registered at the tournament or the hotel. We phoned Harry's office again on Friday and then both decided to get the earliest flight home."

"Okay. How about Monday night?"

"I can't remember doing anything out of the ordinary that night. I packed on Tuesday. I didn't really do anything special. I live alone, except for Jason. You already said you're insisting on talking to him. I give him a home and a damned good allowance in exchange for a number of chores — housework, painting, a bit of gardening. There's a lot to do to maintain an old place like this."

"He was around at the time of the Lache murders, right?"

"Yes, he was."

"Okay," said Fraser. "Continue with your story. You were about to tell me what you were doing that Monday night."

"That's a hell of a long time ago. I was probably watching TV or reading. That's what I do at night. I don't have a computer. I don't surf or play bridge on the internet."

"Can you recall anything significant about the actions of Rob Johnson or Beth Harper on that Monday?"

"Not really. It's a long time ago. Thursday and Friday are branded on my memory, both days. We tried everything to make contact. But I've lost most of Monday and Tuesday."

"Did you talk to Ron or Beth on that Monday?"

"Let's see. I called Johnson to see when he was going to San Antonio. He had a late afternoon flight on Thursday. I had no reason to call Beth."

"You didn't want to execute any trades that day?"

"If I'd wanted to, I wouldn't have called her. I usually talked to Harry or Ron. Never her."

"There was nothing going on that night that might be related to the case?"

"If I think of anything, I'll let you know. Right now, it's a big blank."

Fraser offered grim thanks to Lugner, reminded him to have Jason visit the police station next morning and left to get updates from his colleagues and to share his report.

CHAPTER 15

The trio sat around a table in the sparse meeting room at the police station in Erieville. Stan and Brad suppressed smiles as Art grimaced at the hard oak chairs and went in search of some padding. Brad rounded up three cups of coffee, left over from the day's regular consumption, and they reviewed the day's events.

"We drew a blank at the stores. All the clerks and gas attendants are pretty new. Nobody's been around very long," said Stan.

Brad said, "I'm thinking that the video tapes at the bridge could be a lead. They've got records. I don't know how good they are. The man in charge says if we show up about four-thirty, he'll explain the setup and let us look at everything."

"That'll be a big waste of time," said Stan. "We must have better things to do."

"We can at least look," said Fraser. "We need some hard facts if we're going to get anywhere. I found a few inconsistencies in what people told us. Mainly gossip items. One of these three people, Beth, Johnson or Lugner, has to be our murderer. They all had a motive. Revenge or personal gain."

"That's if you want to discount the possibility of Gehl or the Dinde woman. They each had a motive as well," Stan added.

"Lucy never had much of a reason to kill either of the Laches," said Brad.

"How about being cheated?" asked Stan. "How about being dropped as a girl-friend?"

Fraser interrupted. "I don't see Gehl as a strong possibility either. He and Lucy certainly had opportunity, but they had very little reason to kill a neighbor."

Stan gave him a long look after this statement. "If you say so."

Fraser continued, "I agree that we can't rule them out completely. You always find an odd nut case who turns out to be a killer. But I do believe we ought to focus on the three in Erieville. All had significant reasons to do away with the Laches. All had opportunity. All were physically capable of doing the whole job — the killing, dragging the bodies, burying them."

"Do you think the woman could have done all that?" asked Stan.

"Ever shake hands with her?" replied Fraser.

"Of course I did," replied Stan, glaring.

"She'd crush your fingers if you weren't careful. She could do the necessary physical act, without a doubt. Would she? Did she? Those are other matters."

They sat quietly, immersed in their own thoughts for a few moments until Brad looked at his watch and said, "I say we head for the bridge. Let's cross our fingers that we find something."

Fraser looked at Stan and said, "Why don't we go in your BMW?"

"Will it go that far?" asked Brad.

"Anywhere your Ford will," snapped Stan. "I've got more horses than he has," he announced proudly, nodding towards Fraser. "And that was before I changed the cam sprockets."

"I'd love a ride," said Fraser. He noted that the car was a 1990 model with over 200,000 miles on it. The machine was sparkling clean and purred nicely. The trip took them less than twenty minutes. Stan could not resist a dig at Brad as they stepped out of the car. "You'll have to walk the rest, Brad."

Macvey led the way to the bridge authority office and introduced himself to a middle-aged man who identified himself as Walter Price.

Walter said, "You brought your third man along to help out," he said, nodding at Fraser. "You must be looking into the Hills' murder."

Macvey nodded assent.

"It was on the news today. I hope we can be of help. Now, what exactly are you looking for?"

"We want to look at the Saturday just passed. April Fool's Day," Macvey answered. "That's the night the couple was murdered on the island. Nobody we've talked to so far wants to admit to seeing anything during daylight. We're guessing the murders happened at night. The bodies were discovered Sunday morning."

"All right. We can get those tapes."

"First of all, show us how all your stuff here is organized," suggested Brad. Price took the officers to the room where video records were kept. It looked huge, with stacks of videotapes filed in neat rows along the walls and down the middle of the room.

"We're going digital in a couple of years," Price explained. "When Albany coughs up the money. It'll make this kind of job much easier. Now, let me get my manual out and we'll see what we can do." He took a mammoth loose-leaf binder from a cabinet and thumbed through it. "Here we are. Everything's filed by year.

The 2000 files start over here. That's as far back as we go."

Fraser shared a look with his officers. *So no hope of comparing records on the night of the Lache murders,* he thought with regret.

Price continued. "We've got a number for each month, and so on. You said April 1, this year, right?"

"Right," said Brad.

"Here we go, 2004." He pointed to a section of a few hundred tapes and said, "This is where they ought to be, if all's well." He set his binder down and began to pull tapes from the shelf. He looked at their labels and replaced them. "By the way," he said, "If you pull any tapes off the shelf, make sure you put them back in exactly the same place. And just take one file at a time. Please remember to rewind everything. Otherwise —" He stopped himself. "Hell. I can't see where April is supposed to start. March goes up to here." He pointed at a spot on a shelf. "April records should start right after that."

The officers nodded assent. Price eventually located a lot of a dozen tapes that seemed to be what he wanted. "Okay, boys. Here we go. You'll have to go through them yourselves. The exact date and time information is on the tapes, if not on the boxes. We're a little behind on our filing. You may have to do a bit of sorting to get at what you want."

"How do we do that?" asked Brad.

"There's a TV set in the next room," said Price. "It has a VCR on it and you can flip the tapes in, look at them and decide which ones are of interest. The date and time of the tape will come up right at the beginning." Price showed them the machine, flipped it on, and demonstrated the controls. "It's nothing special. Works well, even if it's a bit old. I'll be in my office for another couple of hours if you need anything."

When the police officers were alone, Fraser said, "We'd better all do this together until we're used to it. We'll need to help each other."

They started with a single tape. It had *April 2004* written clearly on the box, but no date or time. They plugged it into the machine and quickly saw the information they were after. April 2, 2004, 8:00 a.m.

"Heck," said Stan. "That was Sunday. We want Saturday. Are we going to have to look at every tape to get the date and time? We could waste a whole year here."

"We only need to look at the first few seconds of each tape," said Brad. "If we get the wrong tape, we just rewind and set it aside. We only have three days of tapes to look through. This won't take long. They probably have one or two tapes each shift, three tapes a day, or else six. We can either get started or bitch all night."

Stan seemed strangely withdrawn throughout this process, but he did his share of the grunt work without complaint. They took out the tapes, one at a time as advised by Price, and flipped them on the screen. Sure enough, there were two tapes each shift and they quickly found one dated Saturday, April 1, 2004. They set up the tape marked 4 p.m. on April 1, and settled in to watch. Making sense of the videos was another matter, but eventually they were able to understand the method in use by the automatic camera. It was focused to capture a picture of the back end of each vehicle just after the barrier, which was raised when the toll was paid.

"Hey," said Brad. "We're only seeing cars come onto the bridge, not the ones going off. They don't pay leaving, just coming onto the island. So, if this is going to help us at all, we'll need a little luck."

"We've needed luck for the past two weeks," grumbled Stan.

"The big event should come when it's dark," said Fraser. "I hope they have some kind of lighting to show up the plates."

They found that if they set the machine on fast forward, they could not see the markings on the license plates. They had to live with the slow speed.

"We may have to watch this two or three times," said Fraser. "This is our tape, for sure. We can't afford to miss out."

"You mean watch both tapes," groaned Stan. "There are two tapes each shift."

Just then, Brad let out an excited cry.

"Hey, there's a plate we know. Stop and go back a bit."

Macvey implemented his own suggestion and played the machine in slow motion. They could clearly see the plate with Beth Harper's license number.

"I'll be damned," said Fraser.

"Let's go get her," said Brad.

"Hang on," said Fraser. "We've got to finish this tape. Both of these tapes, in fact. We're not going to throw away two weeks of solid work by forgetting the last mile of this job. This is the first genuine piece of evidence we've come across. Rev that machine up and let's keep our eyes peeled."

Once again, they settled in to watch. Car after car went through the barrier and they got to the end of the tape without any further frames of interest.

"I'll rewind and load the next one," said Brad. He executed the task and the next four hours of license plates started on the machine. After an hour, another plate showed up.

"Hey, isn't that our friend Lugner?"

Macvey stopped, rewound, and played the tape in slow motion.

"Look at that. That's Lugner," said Fraser.

"The island had lots of visitors that day," said Stan.

"It sure as hell did," said Fraser. "We might as well finish the tape. There's only a bit left now." The officers marked the dates and times on each of the boxes that Price had given them.

"I'm going to volunteer to help them organize their records," said Macvey. "We ought to go over the tapes from the daylight hours as well. We've got a handle on this thing now. We need to know if someone came over during daylight hours, and maybe hung around and did the job after dark."

After another half hour or so, they saw a third vehicle that they recognized.

"That's the Hill's car," said Brad. "That's not surprising. We thought they arrived on the island sometime during the day of the murder."

Shortly after this, they found another car. "That's Johnson's car. The whole frigging town was here on Saturday."

The officers rewound the last tape and made sure all tapes were filed in their correct order. Macvey made a mental note of the spot where the April tapes were located so they could easily access it for evidence at a future date.

"Gents, we've have to stop right here," said Stan.

"What do you mean?" said Fraser.

"There's something you should know. I was with Beth on Saturday afternoon. I had a date with her and we went over to the island. I was in her car."

"You were in her car?"

Piper nodded glumly.

"You had a date with a witness?"

Another nod.

"In fact, you had a date with a potential suspect."

Stan said nothing, but looked downcast.

"I can't believe a detective would cross the line and arrange a date with a suspect in a case that he is investigating. That's grounds for removal from the case. I've seen officers fired for this sort of thing."

"Never mind the lecture. Do what you have to do," said Stan. "I never, ever believed she could have done the murder. I didn't then and don't now. In fact, I'm damned sure now that she didn't do it."

"Why in hell couldn't you tell us that before we started?" Fraser's anger surged. He paused momentarily to reflect and thought of all the effort Stan had put into the investigation. He sat quietly for another few moments and found he had to control himself so as not to burst into laughter. After a moment, he said, "All right. So you had a date with Beth. It's evident that she isn't the one we're looking for. If you can vouch for her coming back from the island with you on Saturday, she has an alibi. She's off the hook."

"I told you the videotapes were going to be a big waste of time," said Stan.

Brad beamed. "Well at least the tapes got us rid of one suspect."

Fraser said, "You're right about that. We're down to two suspects, if we assume that Lucy and Gehl aren't involved. We have to focus on Johnson and Lugner."

CHAPTER 16

Mike Eppler called Fraser at 8:30 the next morning. "Hi, Art. I've got ten pages of data here. There are a lot of pieces missing and I can't make much sense of it. If you know all the players, you may be able to interpret it. How about I send you a document by email and you can look at it while I talk?"

"Okay," said Fraser. "I'll have my two buddies with me and we can all look and listen while you talk."

"Fine," said Mike. "I'll email the file right away. You'll need a photo editor to open it."

"No problem."

"By the way, I've got the soil samples done as well. We can go over them when we've finished the prints."

An hour later, Fraser had the file with fingerprint data opened and printed. Eppler had drafted two columns with the names of those involved in the case, starting with the Hills and the Laches and moving through Beth, Johnson, Lugner, Lucy Dinde and Dan Gehl. Opposite each name was a clear reference to a set of fingerprints, derived from the prints Fraser and Macvey had sent.

Starting on the next page was another longer table, stretching over several pages, specifying locations of the fingerprints on the Lache Cadillac: front seat, driver, and so on. Opposite each of those entries were pictures of prints with comments. The prints from the car were mostly smudged, partially missing and nowhere near as clear as those on the first page. Eppler had commented beside each to indicate his reasoning for a match up. "Left side of pad is identical" or "center of print is exact".

Opposite front seat, driver, he had five entries:

H. Lache, L. Lache, T. Lugner, R. Johnson, B. Harper

Opposite front seat, passenger, Eppler had entered:

L. Lache B. Harper

The entries for the back seat were a jumble and Fraser skipped over them, thinking they were of little use in any case. "Ready to talk to Mike?" he asked his colleagues.

After phone introductions, Mike took over the conversation. "First of all, these prints are pretty old. We're lucky to get anything from four-year-old prints, especially on surfaces like a car interior. The prints on the steering wheel are blurred, as you'd expect. You don't need a complete print to get a positive identification. If part of the pad is clear, and you get a match with a reference, your identification will stand up in court. In this case, there's no doubt that five people, at least, drove the car. Lache and his wife are no surprises — you'd expect to find them. What you make of the other three, I don't know. Then you go to the passenger side and you find only two clear sets. The wife is expected, and the other lady, you have to figure out. A bit of a puzzle to me is, why aren't the two men showing on the passenger side? I mean, why are they driving but never riding with Lache? That seems a bit strange."

"We know Beth Harper was an occasional passenger," said Fraser. "It's not at all clear why she would be driving. Or why Lugner and Johnson would be driving. Of course, we could leap to a simple conclusion and say one of the three drove the car to Florida. That would explain one set, but not any of the others. That would probably wrap up the case, too. But which one? Can you tell anything from the frequency or the position of the prints?"

"Sorry," said Mike. "Looking at old prints from a small, crowded space is tough enough. That's the best I can do."

"What about the soil samples?" asked Stan.

"You need to understand that soil work is not that precise unless you have major differences in your samples, like red soil and gray. The island soil is very acid. That helped a bit, but I can't be exact here. The samples suggest that the Harper vehicle and the Johnson vehicle were on the property where the soil originated. That's the best I can do."

"Okay, Mike. Thanks for all that. We appreciate your help," said Fraser.

As he was hanging up, the receptionist popped her head in and said, "A Jason Wong to see you, Captain Fraser."

"Thanks," said Fraser. "Show him in here. Stan, you had better sit in and take notes."

Stan took out his notebook, as the receptionist showed in a young man of about twenty-two. He had fine features and bore a striking resemblance to his mother, Nori. His hair was jet black and his complexion was flawless. His clothes were clean and neat, but worn and unfashionable.

"Good morning, Jason," said Fraser. "I'm Captain Fraser and this is detective Piper.

"Hi."

Evidently, we're dealing with a man of few words, thought Fraser. *The guy isn't like his mother at all.*

"We're investigating the deaths of Harry and Louise Lache. This happened about four years ago, in July. You may have known them."

Wong was silent.

Fraser tried a more direct approach. "Did you know them?"

"Maybe."

"Here are a couple of pictures," said Fraser, producing enlargements showing the couple. "They were bridge enthusiasts and very good friends of your employer."

Wong inspected the photos and remarked, "Yes, I did know them. I met them a few times."

That's more like it, he thought. "When did you start to work for Mr. Lugner?"

"1998."

"What was the exact date?"

"September first, 1998."

"You were aware of Mr. Lugner's plans to go to San Antonio during July of 1999?"

"That's a long time ago."

"Tell me what you remember about it."

"He went and came back two days later."

"He flew to San Antonio and came back two days later?" asked Fraser.

Wong nodded assent.

"What day did he leave?"

"He left on Thursday morning. Came back Saturday. I was surprised to see him."

"What can you tell us about the Monday night before he left?"

"I don't remember much."

"Try hard," suggested Fraser.

"Just the usual stuff. I made supper. Did the dishes. Probably watched TV a bit. Not much else. I don't play bridge or anything."

"Not like your mother?" asked Fraser.

Wong started at this question. "No, not like her at all. You know her?"

"We've met," said Fraser. "Did Mr. Lugner go out that evening at all?"

"I don't really know. He could go out and I wouldn't know it. I have a couple of rooms upstairs and I don't know what's happening on the first floor."

"Do you like working for him?"

"For me, it's wonderful."

"Why is that?"

"I get paid well. I have a good place to live. I get to eat anything I want. What else is there?"

A hell of a lot, thought Fraser. *This guy is living in a small dream world.* "You must have some hobbies. What do you do with your time?"

"Mr. Lugner bought me the best computer you ever saw. And a bunch of video games," replied Wong. "I'll bet I have the best setup in the whole United States. Nobody could beat it."

"I see," said Fraser. Taking on a more commanding tone of voice, he said, "Look, if you withhold information, you could be charged with a crime yourself. Withholding information is a serious crime, you know. On Monday, July 19, in 1999, two people were killed. Their names were Mr. and Mrs. Lache. You admit you knew them. Last Saturday, two more people were killed on Wellesley Island — Mr. and Mrs. Hill. It so happens that they were also good friends of your boss, Mr. Lugner. We need to gather all the facts we can about these murders. The dates I'm interested in are the evening back in 1999, and last Saturday."

"I'm not withholding anything. That was a long time ago. I didn't know there was a murder until just a few days ago. There was nothing special about that time in 1999. It was summer. I did my job. I cooked. I cleaned the kitchen at night, did chores during the day, maybe played some video, watched TV or read a book. That's all."

"All right," Fraser said, finally. "Let's leave it at that. How about last Saturday?"

"Just a regular day. I did my jobs around the house, that's all."

"How about Mr. Lugner? Did he do anything unusual on Saturday?"

"I don't keep track of him. He's around at mealtimes. We work together on projects when he wants something done. I don't look after his calendar."

"If you remember anything and want to talk to us, give us a call."

Jason left quietly.

Fraser stood at the front of the tiny room that provided space for meetings at the Erieville police station. He had mounted a large pad of paper on the wall behind him and held a marker in his left hand as he faced Macvey and Piper.

"Back to school," said Brad.

"Ready, professor," added Stan.

"Never mind that stuff," said Fraser, smiling. "Let's make some sense of all this. We have Beth's and Johnson's prints on the steering wheel of the Cadillac. We've got soil verification from the Lache lot on Wellesley Island on both Beth's and Johnson's cars. We've got Lugner and Johnson's license plates showing up on films the day of the Hill's murders. Casanova here says he can vouch for Beth on the day of the murder, so we rule her out. Forget the fact that she went over to the island the day the Hill couple were murdered and that she drove Lache's Cadillac."

Fraser wrote out a table of notes on the pad as he talked.

	Beth	Ron	Lugner	Lucy	Gehl
fingerprints	~~Y~~	Y	Y	N	N
video	~~Y~~	Y	Y	N	N
soil samples	~~Y~~	Y	N	N	N

"You might strike out Lucy and Gehl as well. We're pretty sure they're not involved," said Macvey. "They don't show up anywhere, and their fingerprints aren't on Lache's car. We're down to Johnson and Lugner."

"We have no soil samples showing on Lugner's car," Stan proclaimed. "That suggests he may not have visited the property on the weekend. Maybe we're down to one single culprit, Mr. Johnson."

"The soil samples aren't positive," Fraser warned. "They could be old samples from anywhere on the island."

Stan reddened.

Brad agreed. "We have more work to do. It's time we put a little heat on Johnson and old Lugner."

"You want to borrow Lucy's shovel?" suggested Stan, smirking.

"Maybe. But we need to know what the hell they were doing on the island on Saturday. Picnicking in April? What were you doing, Stan?"

Stan reddened once again. "It was a beautiful day. We went for a drive."

"Stop anywhere?" asked Brad, rolling his eyes.

"We stopped for lunch. Let's get back to work here. I say Johnson did it," said Stan. "Lugner is too old to drag bodies around. Johnson could be stronger than he looks and he had the motive."

"Let's stick to the facts," barked Fraser. "We're all rambling around. We can't arrest anyone today. What's missing? The trouble with my chart there is that not a single item is conclusive. All we get from the soil samples is an indicator. All you get from the fingerprints is an idea of who drove the car, not when. And the videos we saw tell us that Beth and Lugner and Johnson drove over to the island at some time on the date the Hills' murder took place. I call it slippery evidence. Not a single one of our so-called clues would stand up in court. The D.A. wouldn't even think about taking the case to court with what we've got."

"Brad's right," Stan said. "The next step has to be to talk with Lugner and Johnson and get them to tell us what they were doing on the island that day."

"There's one big item we're missing," said Fraser.

"What's that?" asked Macvey.

"Who owned the barn that got blown down? We haven't heard from Wooler." He got up and added a line to his chart.

Stan pointed out, "Whoever's name gets ticked off in that box is the person we're after."

When Fraser called Fort Meade, the receptionist told him that Wooler was out of town and would be back the next day.

— —

First thing next morning, the officers gathered at the Erieville police station and Fraser again placed a call to Wooler.

"Hi," said Wooler. "We made some progress on your ownership problem."

"Great. Tell me about it."

"We got the property nailed down to a guy in Erieville. Name of Lugner."

"Lugner," said Fraser. "Thanks a million." He hung up and turned to the others with a grin.

"Lugner," he repeated. "He owns the property where the Cadillac was found." The room was like a tomb for several moments, as the officers realized that they had broken the case.

"Lugner," said Macvey. "That son of a bitch."

"Now, how do we wrap this up?" asked Fraser. "How do we tie Lugner to the car beyond a reasonable doubt? The fact that the car was stored on property that he owned pretty well nails it down. If we can show conclusively that he traveled down to that area, or back, at the time of the murders, we have the case tied up with a ribbon."

"He must have driven the car down there and found a different way to get home. What would that be? Fly, bus, two cars down and one back?" wondered Macvey.

Fraser interrupted. "Before we get into that, I'd better get hold of the D.A. We haven't dialed her into our thinking yet. We need to make sure we get the evidence she needs. We don't want to miss something really important." Fraser called a number on his cell phone and left a message for Diana Westbury to call.

"Lugner would have flown back here, landing in Syracuse and driving home. We could check all the flights from Orlando to Syracuse. We should look at Tampa to Syracuse as well. There aren't many airlines that make that flight. I went through the list when I booked my flight to Florida. He'd have five choices — Delta, US Air, Northwest, American, and Continental. We're probably looking at the same airlines for the flight from Syracuse to San Antonio," said Macvey.

"Not asking much, are we, to get five airlines to go over passenger lists from five years ago," said Stan. "If they don't have good computer records, we're dead."

"Let's worry about that if and when we come to it," Fraser snapped.

"We have the dates when he most probably flew. It would take him a few days, two or three anyway to drive down there with the stolen car. We can check all the flights on the days in that window," Macvey said. "He'd stash the car and either fly or drive back."

Fraser broke in. "No, we've got it wrong. It didn't quite work that way. Lugner was in San Antonio on the Thursday of the Lache murders, remember? He met Johnson there. They looked all over, or acted out some kind of script that made it look like they were searching for the Laches."

"All right," said Brad. "How about this. Maybe he's lying and didn't fly down to San Antonio from Syracuse like he said. Nobody checked on him. Johnson said they never flew together. He could have roared down to Florida in the Caddie and flown to San Antonio from there."

"All we have is Lugner's word that he flew from Syracuse," said Stan.

"Interesting," said Fraser. "We need a record proving that Lugner flew from Syracuse to San Antonio, like he said. Otherwise, it would look like he got to San Antonio some other way."

"If he flew to San Antonio from either Syracuse or Florida," pointed out Macvey, "we have a problem."

"What's that?" asked Fraser.

"If he flew from Syracuse, where did he hide the Caddie while he was in San Antonio?"

"He has a big three car garage at his place. He uses it for one car and a supply of firewood. He could easily pull another car in there when it's dark and take it out the same way. Nobody would need to know about it."

"Makes sense," said Macvey. "That means the kid would have to know about it. Maybe he went along on the trip to Florida and helped with the driving. We never took his prints, so we can't say for sure that he didn't drive."

"Why don't we just ask Lugner point blank how he got to San Antonio, whether it was a direct flight or a trip from Florida?" said Stan.

Fraser replied, "We're not ready to approach Lugner directly. I'd prefer to have as many facts in our hands as possible and leave him no chance to be evasive. We may be able to narrow this down. I'll call Johnson to see if he can tell us which airline Lugner took."

When Fraser called the Lache Investments' office, he got hold of Beth, and she turned out to be very helpful. "Ron always uses American. He has a frequent flyer account with them. I booked the flight, in fact. I know that Ted uses Delta for some reason. He probably collects points from them."

Stan went ahead with his call, grateful for the simplification.

Meanwhile, Brad took on the job of calling Wooler down in Fort Meade to ask him to talk to people in the neighborhood of the Lugner property. He took the liberty of advising Wooler that he would probably be down in Fort Meade for another visit within the next few days. Fraser thought, *he's still interested in his golf career.*

When Diana Westbury called, Fraser went over the highlights of the investigation. She listened carefully as he reviewed the information they had on finding the car, the barn that was demolished, the ownership of the property, and their thinking on pinning down the travel arrangements. She supported the direction his team was taking and proceeded to ask her own questions.

"I'm curious about the young hired fellow Lugner has working for him. He seems to be pretty thick with Lugner, from what you've told me. I'll bet you he knows a lot more than he's letting on."

"I agree. Jason must know facts that he's not telling us. For instance, if Lugner hid the Cadillac in his garage, even for a short time, Jason probably knew about it."

"I'm also wondering about the events in Florida," Diana continued. "How did Lugner get from the barn to an airport? If Lugner had another driver, it would have to be someone he knew pretty well. The other guy would never forget a trip like that. It would seem like a pointless trip and Lugner would need a pretty good story to explain it all. An accomplice would facilitate all the connections Lugner had to make," she said. "He would need someone to drive him to an airport or wherever he was going after locking the Cadillac in the barn. Maybe they had two cars, for all we know. Two of them could have driven down in two cars, and then brought one car back."

"We were thinking along that line, but if we trace the airline tickets, we don't have to worry about driving and the possibility of two cars."

"True. You're on the right track," she said. "There'd be a car rental at the other end, no doubt."

Fraser said, "If we can prove he was in Florida at all, it's condemning. If we get a positive link showing Lugner traveled back to Syracuse from Florida at the right time, I'd like to arrest him. If we tie Wong in somehow, I'll arrest both."

"That sounds right."

They exchanged pleasantries and hung up.

CHAPTER 17

The following morning, the Delta manager at Syracuse called Stan Piper to let him know that a Ted Lugner had flown from Syracuse to San Antonio on July 22 and returned on July 24. He had also flown from Tampa to Syracuse on July 28, accompanied by a Jason Wong. "Bingo," shouted Stan, as he hung up the phone and relayed the news to his colleagues.

"Let's go," said Macvey, more excited than he had been for the past three weeks.

"Okay," Fraser responded. "We've got what we need now to make an arrest, and everything the D.A. wanted."

Fraser decided that he wanted all members of his team to be present at the arrest. It was evident from Macvey's excitement that his colleagues would get satisfaction out of participating in the final chapter of the case they had worked on so hard. There was also a safety factor in appearing with backup, although he didn't expect any problems with Lugner.

"Let's go," he said. "Let's all go."

They climbed into Stan's old BMW and hustled over to Lugner's place. Fraser reminded them that he expected to do all the talking, Stan was to keep complete records of all conversation and Macvey was to keep a watchful eye on Lugner in case he tried anything foolish. After unsuccessful tries with the doorbell, they went around the house and found Lugner lounging in his backyard. He showed little surprise at seeing the delegation.

Lugner said, "More damned questions, I suppose." He did not rise from his chair, and appeared calm and in control of his emotions. "What can I do for you?"

Fraser said, "You are under arrest for the murder of Harry and Louise Lache. I'm going to read you your rights. I expect we will also charge you with the murder of the Hills, but that will come later."

Lugner reddened and exploded with a roar. "You don't have to read me my rights. You can get the hell off my property, right now. Talk to my lawyer. I'm done talking to you jokers." He rose and made violent gestures as he spoke.

Fraser said, "You can call your lawyer from the station. Get your coat and whatever you might need. You're about to be a guest of the state for some time.

We also need to talk to Wong. He was involved in your crimes and we intend to arrest him for it."

The deep red color in Lugner's face drained to a pale shade of white. He seemed to stumble, caught himself, and muttered, with an air of uncertainty, "Why in hell would you want to arrest the boy?"

"We have the Lache Cadillac from your property in Fort Meade. You drove the car down there and intended to hide it for some time. One of the hurricanes knocked your barn down and left the car in the open for everyone to see. We have records of two airline tickets from Tampa to Syracuse, one for Lugner and one for Wong. Both tickets were dated the week of the Lache murders."

Lugner availed himself of the nearest chair and sat down. He stared at the ground for several moments. He raised his eyes to meet Fraser's and said, "You've got to leave the boy out of this completely. He did nothing wrong. He only followed my instructions. Please don't lay any charges against him. He's a good lad."

"The D.A. has already authorized a warrant for his arrest," replied Fraser.

Lugner heaved a sigh, "The damned barn." He sat quietly, collecting his thoughts. "You can't involve Jason in any of this," he pleaded. "I'm an old man. I have little to lose anyway. You know damned well that if I give you a full confession, you save the state tens of thousands of dollars in legal and court costs. You wrap up the case in weeks, not years. Surely you can see the practicality of it. Jason had nothing to do with any of the crimes. Leave him out of this. Completely."

"That's the D.A.'s call. I don't have that authority," said Fraser.

"He just did what I asked him, so maybe he's a minor accessory. The D.A. should understand that. Call your bloody D.A. I'll cooperate with you if you leave him alone."

"What do you mean by cooperate?" asked Fraser.

"I'll consider a full confession," said Lugner.

"You're waffling."

"Like hell. You'll get what you want. Just tear up the warrant for his arrest."

"All right. I'll make the call," said Fraser.

Fraser drummed his fingers on the arm of his chair. He asked to go into the kitchen alone, phoned Diana Westbury, and was thankful that he got her on the second ring. He explained the situation to her and she agreed readily to Fraser's proposal.

When he returned, he announced, "We're all set. We'll take a statement, you sign it, and we won't arrest Jason." Lugner seemed relieved, nodded agreement, and all five men arranged themselves in more or less comfortable positions on the patio.

"You might wonder at what kind of situation might lead to murder in a setting like the game of bridge, where folks are generally friendly. The worst that happens is normally a few insults fly across the table, a display of temper, maybe a breakup of a friendship, or sometimes a marriage. There's only one supposed killing in the history of crime that authorities attribute to the game of bridge, and it simultaneously ended a marriage and the life of a player.

"In my case, we had a situation where a partnership developed and we got some pretty good results. Harry and I became fast friends and a team evolved that had loads of fun and did pretty well at the table.

"Then something snapped. Harry couldn't say a civil word to me. He kidded me every time he saw me. And that goddamned laugh of his. Then Louise got on my case. She was subtle. She never said anything directly, but she made allusions to my sexual orientation. She found ways to hurt me, and compounded the hurt by laughing at her own jokes. It got so I couldn't stand it.

"Harry and I were making fools of each other. We argued and said stupid things to one another every time we sat down. We went on and on. I'm sure we bothered the hell out of other people at the table."

"So you couldn't stand either Harry or Louise any longer," said Fraser.

"Louise contrived these jokes that always made me feel awkward. The more she pressed me, the worse I felt about myself. Instead of our old, happy-go-lucky relationship, we were a trio of hate and spite.

"For many of us, bridge is a way to overcome feelings of inadequacy in earlier life. You learn to play the game and you get feelings of competence. When you do something good, people around the table give you recognition for it. We had a lot of success at the bridge table, and our whole group showed a lot of mutual recognition in the early days.

"After a while, Johnson started to take all the credit for our success. People thought of us as hacks and him as the expert.

When we went to a tournament, he did everything he could to get his hands written up in daily bulletins, nobody else's. His name got to be well known and the rest of us got none of the credit. That bothered me a bit, but not as much as the teasing that flew around. I couldn't stand that.

"The whole business ate at my insides. Time passed and I found ways to get at Harry, and to some extent, at Louise as well. I was pretty good at sly digs, particularly at the area that hurt him most, his sexual prowess. That really began to damage our relationship. I started to talk about Harry's kid — how he couldn't have children with Louise, but just picked someone off the street and had a kid with her. That got to both of them. It almost broke them up. All of this digging at each other was destroying the three of us, our self worth."

"Why couldn't you just walk away?" asked Fraser.

"To what?" countered Lugner. "My life was all wrapped up with the Laches. We were together at tournaments, together in the summers at the island. He handled all my investments. We had been through so much together that it was easier to just keep going. I got to be more and more bitter about the fact that I'd ever entered into a relationship with them. I'm an old man. What in hell was I supposed to do with my life at eighty? I have no family. I've lived in Erieville for years. I felt powerless, frustrated. Then I finally reached a breaking point and felt I couldn't go any further. I hatched this plot. Murder was the only way out. It became the only way I could see of ending all the torture they were causing me. I couldn't think of anything to say to them that would stop the flow of insults and demeaning comments. No quick repartee ever came to mind during or after one of our tirades.

"The only answer was to permanently silence the foul mouth that was the source of all my anguish. I began to hatch plots to shut them up. I thought of drowning, shooting, poisoning, all of the means that I had read about in books or seen in films. They started out as harmless daydreams, going nowhere. None of these seemed adequate. I started to see him dead, eyes closed, complexion pale, and best of all, mouth permanently shut. Eventually, I realized that I would have to get rid of Louise along with him. Harry and Louise were always together, except when Harry played golf. That complicated matters. I needed a quick way to end them both and dispose of the bodies.

"The idea that I had a plan of action lifted my spirits. I could accept the sarcasm and the laughter. Then San Antonio came along and I had a perfect opportunity."

"And the Hills?" asked Fraser.

Lugner sighed and shifted his weight in the chair. "I thought I'd committed a perfect crime. The night I buried the Laches, I took the bodies up to Wellesley Island. I drove onto the property and parked. There were no lights on anywhere near the place. When I was in the Cadillac, all set to leave, a car came driving down the road and turned into the property. Both of the Hills were in the car. They had a clear view of the Cadillac. It was dark, but they would figure out it was Harry's after a bit. They might have thought Harry was driving when they first saw the car, but I was sure they'd be able to identify me even if we didn't talk to each other. We knew each other pretty well, and sooner or later they'd put everything together. I got out of there as fast as I could. As long as the Laches stayed buried, I had no worries about them. But when the construction crew discovered the bodies, I had to act."

Fraser said, "When the Lache bodies were found, you had to deal with the Hills."

"They knew everything. They would have pieced it all together in a second. The perfect crime almost came off. If the Hills were questioned, I was done."

EPILOGUE

Fraser phoned ahead to tell Karen that he would not arrive until around ten that night. She prepared a light meal, bathed, and donned a soft, silk dressing gown in his favorite color. When she greeted him with her usual warm embrace, she found him distant.

"Uh oh," she said. "What's the matter? Aren't you happy about your case?"

"Oh yeah. It's all finished. We had Lugner cold and he ended up confessing."

"Congratulations! You wrapped up a quadruple murder in two weeks. That's unheard of. I'll open a bottle of Cava for you and we'll celebrate."

"I guess we should. I'm a little annoyed right now, to tell you the truth."

Karen steered him over to a straight-backed chair and began a spirited massage of his tight shoulder and neck muscles.

"Oh, that's nice."

"Tell me the whole truth."

"I get the feeling I've been jerked around. They order me up there to Wellesley Island and tell me to do a professional job. They load me up with Stan for an assistant. He's not a detective. He should never have been on the payroll. I have the rank of captain, but they gave me no choice in the matter."

"Would you have solved it faster with someone else?" asked Karen.

"It's not that. I'm getting to hate the politics of the force. It's frustrating."

Karen ended her energetic kneading and walked to the fridge. She pulled out a bottle and popped the cork while Art was sulking. She poured a glass of champagne for him and a glass of ginger ale for herself while she talked. "Don't you think people will acknowledge what you've done? Last time we talked, you said you liked the young guy. Macvey?"

"He was okay."

"You said he was a bit of a country boy, but you thought he had real talent, that this was good experience for him. He might have learned something from the master."

"That part of it's fine. As a matter of fact, I'd work with him anytime. He's young and a lot smarter than he appears. But Bryder and Cameron are going to take all the credit for this case and all they did was push me around."

"They were doing their job," said Karen. "That's what they get paid for — assigning the right men to the right chores."

"The way they did it eats at me. I have half a notion to resign and start my own agency."

"That might be fun. You think it would be less frustrating than working for the folks you know?"

"There's really only one way to find out."

"That would mean two big changes to your lifestyle."

"Two?"

"You're going to be a father!"

"A what? You're —"

Karen nodded and smiled.

Fraser sat silently, enjoying the feeling of total satisfaction that crept over him. *There are pluses,* he thought.

IF YOU ENJOYED THIS BOOK, BE SURE TO PICK UP THE FIRST ART FRASER BRIDGE MYSTERY!

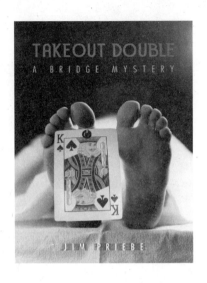

TAKEOUT DOUBLE:

A BRIDGE MYSTERY

by Jim Priebe

1-894154-89-4

Master Point Press

A delightful bridge mystery — polished, suspenseful, and thoroughly enjoyable.
- ABTA Quarterly

If you are looking for something different for a change, then your search may be over. I read very little fiction, so the fact that I read the book from cover to cover is praise in itself. Indeed, once I had started it took only a few days to finish.
- Julian Pottage

Bob Smithers is dead, although few in the bridge world will shed any tears.

Art Fraser, the ambitious police lieutenant assigned to the case, knows the bridge world well. He reckons that should give him the inside track on cracking his first homicide investigation, the one that will bring him the promotion he wants so much. But Smithers made enemies easily, both at the bridge table and away from it, and Art has plenty of potential murderers to investigate. Even his own bridge friends have to be treated as suspects, and he begins to uncover a complex tangle of jealousy, ambition, sex, and deceit amongst people to whom he knows bridge is far more than just a game.

Then a second body shows up…